The Magnetic Mindset:

365 Ways to Attract Abundance

Valerie Dawson

FORWARD

Congratulations! You are on your way to creating a magnetic mindset so that you can attract a future filled with abundance.

I recommend that you start with the first section of the book that reviews the Law of Attraction and how it affects you financially. You will learn some valuable lessons to get started right away to start creating a brighter future.

Then you will discover 365 more pages that each contain a success quote, thought for the day and affirmation – all designed to help you to unlock your power to manifest abundance.

Utilize these powerful processes at your own pace. You may choose to read one page each day or you may prefer to read several in one sitting.

Take some time to consider how the insights apply to your own life. Practice each success lesson to dissolve away your obstacles and open the flow of abundance. Then, solidify your mindset shift by focusing on the joyful affirmation throughout the day.

By feeding your mind with these words of love, success, abundance and ease, you'll soon notice a shift in energy, which will open the window to new opportunities. With a little practice, the changes that you are making in your mindset will soon create more abundance in your life.

You are a talented deliberate creator. So start making your dreams a reality… today is your new beginning!

What is the Law of Attraction & How Does it Affect Me Financially?

You're probably used to thinking of money as a tangible object that resides in your wallet and bank account until you're ready to use it. You pay bills with it, purchase products and services with it, and maybe even donate some of it to worthwhile charities.

Where does this money come from? If you're like most people, you probably have a job or business through which you exchange time, products or services for money. This is the most common way to receive money, but did you know you can also attract it with the Law of Attraction?

Have you ever wondered why some people have a lot of money and others have so little? You may be tempted to say that the former group must work hard and the latter group doesn't, but that's not always true either, is it? There are plenty of people who work VERY hard but still barely manage to make ends meet each month. There are also plenty of people who don't work at all, yet have millions of dollars in the bank.

Assuming that both groups have the same potential for opportunities, the difference between them is usually a little something called: MINDSET.

One group has a wealth mindset and the other group has a lack mindset. The Law of Attraction is activated by your mindset – in other words, the things you think and feel on a regular basis.

Here's how it works: Your thoughts trigger your emotions. Your emotional state emits a specific "frequency" of energy to the universe, and the universe returns events and experiences into your life, that correspond with your emotional frequency.

When you think and feel positively on a regular basis, everything in your life seems to "flow" more easily, including money. When your thoughts and emotions lean more toward the negative side on a regular basis, you experience more problems, setbacks and financial lack in your life.

Also important are your beliefs. Your beliefs form the structure of what is possible for you. If you believe you have to work hard to have a lot of money, you'll create exactly that experience for yourself. If you don't believe you deserve more than a certain amount of money, you'll block more from arriving! Whatever your beliefs are, they are your TRUTH, and you will subconsciously create "evidence" that supports that truth over and over again until you learn to do things differently.

The good news is that you can learn to use the Law of Attraction to improve your financial situation, and it will be much easier than you might think!

How Is Lack Formed?

What is lack and how does it appear in your life, anyway?

Lack is the condition of not having something. In other words, lack is the ABSENCE of something. But the absence of exactly "what" may surprise you. Lack is not the absence of money, or health, or love. Those are just the symptoms of lack.

At its core, lack is simply the blockage of ENERGY.

EVERYTHING IS ENERGY! When you experience lack of any kind, you are cutting off the natural flow of energy through your life. This can affect much more than your financial situation. In fact, you may notice that when you lack one thing, you usually lack other things too. Your relationships may be more strained or distant; you may experience poor health, lower energy, financial difficulties, or even appliance or vehicle breakdowns. None of this is a coincidence! When you block the flow of abundance, it can manifest in many different ways.

How does this blockage get started? By focusing on what you do not have, or what you do not want. Though it sounds like a bad joke, lack is formed when you focus continuously on lack!

Every time you worry about your financial situation, agonize over a shortage of money, or feel stressed about your bills, you attract the experience of lack into your life. The more you think about things and experiences you don't have, the more you'll attract an absence or blockage of the things you want.

This creates a nasty cycle that you can remain stuck in for years! Focus on lack, create more lack, which makes you focus even more on lack, which creates even more lack . . . and on it goes indefinitely!

It gets even worse too, because focusing obsessively on the lack in one area of your life can attract lack into other (even unrelated) areas of your life too. Next thing you know your entire life is in a major funk and you have no idea how it got so bad.

If you're stuck in one of these funks right now, don't worry! Turning it around is a simple matter of identifying the things you're doing that are creating more lack, and learning how to focus more on abundance – which we will cover in detail in the next few pages of this book.

For starters, did you know that there are very specific thoughts and emotions that attract lack? It's true!

Thoughts and Emotions that Attract Lack

Are you starting to see how pervasive a focus on lack can be? The more you lend your attention and energy to the existence of lack, the more you fuel it!
What exactly do I mean by "lending your attention and energy to the existence of lack?" There are specific thoughts and emotions that create lack and make it grow stronger in your life.

Here they are, in no particular order:

Fear
Anxiety
Helplessness
Hopelessness
Pessimism
Doubt
Frustration
Worry
Jealousy
Resentment

Every time you choose one of these focuses, you create more lack. In order to turn lack into abundance, you have to AVOID investing in these negative emotions. That's not easy to do, I know. Especially when you're feeling stressed by financial issues, your natural tendency is to obsess over them and try to find a solution. But every time you allow yourself to feel these emotions, you keep making matters worse.

There are two things you can do to prevent these emotions from creating more lack.

First, as I mentioned a moment ago, avoid sinking into feelings like those described above. As soon as you notice yourself starting to feel stressed or worried about money, immediately shift your focus to something else.

You can engage in a bit of self-talk if it helps; say something like, "There's no point worrying about something I can't control, so I'm going to focus on something that makes me feel good." Then spend time on unrelated activities.

I'm not suggesting that you ignore financial crises or shirk your responsibilities. Rather, give these issues the attention they require and do what you can to make them better. If it makes you feel better to get a second job or refinance/consolidate your loans, do it.

But most important is to avoid INVESTING NEGATIVE EMOTIONS into these issues as you work to resolve them. Stay as detached as you can while doing what you have to do.

Secondly, begin directing more positive emotions toward your financial situation. Even if you have to engage in a bit of fantasizing in order to do so, you need to get some positive emotions flowing to attract more abundance!

There are many ways to do this, but one that always works for me is to keep affirming, "I always have more than enough money for everything I need." Just keep saying it over and over again, allowing yourself to feel confident and happy that your financial needs are being met. This is also a good thing to do when you notice you're starting to feel worried or frightened about not having enough money.

Just immediately turn the focus around and say, "I ALWAYS have more than enough money for EVERYTHING I need." (Say it with power and conviction in your voice, and really believe that it is so.)

As you begin shifting your focus from negative emotions to positive emotions, you should start to notice your financial situation shifting to a better place also. You might receive an unexpected check in the mail, you might get a bonus or pay raise at work, or you may even notice you're starting to receive unexpected gifts from other people or companies.

These are great signs that it's working! Keep replacing negative emotions with positive as often as possible and you'll keep the good energy flowing – which will keep inspiring greater and greater change in your life.

Activities that Intensify Lack

Are you starting to feel a shift in your financial situation yet? If not, be sure to keep choosing the positive emotions as often as possible. It may take a little time to notice changes taking place, but the end result is well worth it!

Today we're going to cover some destructive habits and activities that contribute to lack, and offer helpful suggestions for turning them around.

To start, I'd like to ask you a question: How do you treat your money?

If money was a person in your life, would he or she feel honored and loved; or abused, neglected and disrespected?

Ouch. If you're like most people, your relationship with money could probably use a little tender loving care. Attracting more money into your life means learning to treat money with respect and kindness.

I know, you're thinking, "What, respect and kindness for an inanimate object? Why?"

Because money is NOT an inanimate object at all! It is energy, remember? Even more importantly, it is a projection of YOUR energy. That means it is a part of you, and it has a life and intelligence all its own.

If someone treated you the way you treat your money, you probably wouldn't stick around for more abuse, would you? Money won't either.

Therefore, it is crucial to avoid these habits and activities where your money is concerned:

Excessive spending

Excessive debt
Reckless disregard for the importance of
money
No savings plan
Financial disorganization
Poor planning

You see, the problem isn't that you don't have
enough money. The true problem is that you
are not managing your money in a way that
attracts more of it!

Here are the best things you can do to begin
honoring your money (and attracting more!).

Begin a savings plan immediately. It doesn't
matter if you can only spare a dollar or two
each week, but begin setting aside money into
a savings account right away. And do not
touch that money for ANY reason! This step is
very important because it puts you into the
mindset of "having money" – even if the
amount you have isn't a lot yet. The more you
do this, the wealthier you're going to feel as
you remember that you're not "living on the
edge".

Avoid spending money on anything that
doesn't contribute VALUE to your life. Do you
really need that cute purse when you've
already got a closet full of them? Do you really
need more "toys" that will only gather dust
when you tire of them in a few weeks?

Instead, begin spending your money on things that will help you to grow and deepen as an individual. Buy books to expand your knowledge. Invest in business courses or career development programs. Better yet, begin contributing money to investment programs so it can grow and eventually work FOR you.

This doesn't mean you can't enjoy the occasional treat. You can still enjoy nice things, but be very choosy about what they are and how often you buy them.

Get organized. If you haven't balanced your checkbook in ages, or you have no idea how much debt you have, figure it out and create a plan for paying it off. The point of this exercise is not to make you feel bad, but to take responsibility for your financial situation. Trust me - you'll feel much better when you have a clear understanding of where you stand right now, and a solid plan for getting somewhere better.

Those should keep you busy for a little while! Remember, you don't have to do everything all at once. Starting small is okay. Eventually it all adds up!

Forming a Magnetic Mindset to Attract Abundance

An abundance mindset is pretty much the opposite of a lack mindset, and it's easy to switch from one to the other – with a little conscious choice.

There are three main steps I'd suggest in order to create an abundance mindset:

Give all of your attention and energy to abundance. Remember in a previous email I said you needed to avoid contributing energy and emotion to lack? Now you've got to start giving all the energy and emotion you can to abundance!

Here's how: As often as you can, keep aware of the abundance surrounding you. Look at your home and all the possessions within it, and marvel at how wealthy you really are. Feel grateful for all you have, and affirm that more is on the way.

Also be sure to notice abundance in the world around you. See how nature blooms and grows so effortlessly, and gaze in awe at store shelves that are loaded with anything you could ever want! Abundance is everywhere if you simply open your eyes to it!

Believe it's possible to have more than you can imagine. You're probably used to thinking of your financial situation in very limited ways. You earn money from a job or business, but you can't see any other way for money to come to you. Acknowledge daily that the universe has UNLIMITED options for sending more money into your life. Decide on a sum of money you'd like to receive in the near future, and then begin affirming that it is on the way to you. Don't worry about HOW it will arrive. Just believe that it will find a way to enter your life.

Expect to receive. Your expectations are very powerful! If you expect to have a limited amount of money, that's exactly what will happen. Instead, start expecting more money to come to you from many different sources. Affirm daily, "Today I expect great things to happen! Money, success and abundance in all forms will find their way to me effortlessly and quickly!" Then be on the lookout for great opportunities – and grab them when they arrive!

Do you see how easy it is to shift your focus from lack to abundance now? It's really just a matter of what you choose to focus on and invest in emotionally. However, there are also specific actions you can take that will help too.

Activities that Increase Abundance

Now you now know what NOT to do if you want to avoid creating more lack, and you've learned some simple mental and emotional techniques that can help attract more abundance into your life.

Now I'd like to share a few tips about physical actions that can begin attracting more abundance into your life.

Do what you love. The more time you spend feeling GOOD, the more positive emotion you contribute to the creation of your life. This is true in relation to your financial situation, but also ALL other areas of your life.

Be sure to make a habit of doing the things you really LOVE to do. This can be everything from creative pursuits to reading inspiring books; spending quality time with friends and family, and making your own self-care a high priority. If it makes you feel light, happy, fulfilled and relaxed, do it as often as possible!

Open gateways for prosperity to enter your life. Are you doing everything you can to help the universe send more money your way? Or are you disallowing abundance by refusing to take action? The universe can find many ways to boost your abundance, but it can do so much more easily if YOU take action to invite greater opportunities! Possible action steps might include: applying for a better paying job, buying a lottery ticket, networking with successful people, sharing your talents and skills with the world, and anything else that will create an opening for abundance to enter your life.

Most importantly, do these things without attaching specific expectations to them. Instead, allow the actions themselves to be fun and enjoyable. Do them because you enjoy doing them, without expecting them to pay off in any other way. When you do this, you are "allowing" lots of great things into your life – including money and abundance in many forms.

Don't worry about the "how". We're so used to trying to figure everything out on our own that it can be hard to detach from "how" abundance will come to you. Don't try to brainstorm money-making activities or focus obsessively on how to bring in more money. Instead, let the universe work on your behalf. Decide how much money you'd like to have in the immediate future, and then ask the universe to lead you to the best opportunities for attracting it. Not only will you discover better opportunities than you could hunt down on your own, you'll probably enjoy them much more too!

These three steps may seem very simple, (name), but they hold great power because they send a strong message to the universe that you are ready, willing and open to receiving greater abundance into your life – without grasping desperately at it.

Shifting Into an Abundant Reality

By now you've got a solid idea of the thoughts, emotions and actions that you should avoid at all costs in order to banish lack from your life forever. You've also got some clear, simple steps you can begin taking right away to begin attracting more abundance into your life.

But did you know that you can instantly create change by simply SHIFTING INTO AN ABUNDANT REALITY?

Here's what I mean by that. Right now, you are living FROM a specific reality. Since you are reading this book, I'm going to assume that your reality isn't exactly what you want it to be. You don't have as much money as you'd like to have, and perhaps you've got lack in other areas too. In your mind, this is your "truth" – it's the perspective you live FROM in every moment of every day. Right?

But what if you could change this perspective simply by changing your mindset? You can!

You can do this by simply thinking, feeling and acting like you would if your reality were different.

How would you think, feel and act if you had all the money you wanted? How would you think, feel and act if you were successful, happy and content with your life?

I bet it would be different than you think, feel and act right now! Am I right?

Starting immediately, I want to encourage you to think, feel and act like a person who is already living the life you want to be living. Make list of words that describe how you would feel in this new reality.

Examples:

Happy
Secure
Wealthy
Content
Confident
Fulfilled
Passionate
Alive
Joyful
Grateful
Relaxed
Peaceful

Keep this list of words handy, and then start thinking, feeling and acting that way as often as possible!

Now, keep in mind that you'll probably feel strange doing this at the beginning. It will feel almost like you're acting in a play, or like you are lying to yourself. That's normal, because your current self-image won't match up to the new self-image you're trying to adopt. That's okay!

The more you do this, the more comfortable you're going to get with it, and eventually your physical circumstances are going to start shifting in a new direction. Believe me, it works!

Just keep at it as often as you can, consciously choosing to live FROM your new reality. BECOME the person who is living the life you want to be living, and you will create that life for yourself.

More than anything else, the one thing I want you to take away from this book is the fact that using the Law of Attraction to improve ANY area of your life is as simple as learning to think, feel and act in different ways.

The way your life is right now is not an accident. It resulted from very specific things you did to create your circumstances. I'm not saying that to make you feel badly, but rather to show you that you DO have the power to choose different, BETTER circumstances too!

Knowing what you know now, you can use your magnetic mindset to create the life of your dreams.

Wishing you great abundance and all good things,

Valerie Dawson, MSW, CHt
Founder of The Dawson Method
www.MagneticMindset.com

Day 1

Take the first step in faith. You don't have to see the whole staircase. Just take the first step.

- Martin Luther King, Jr.

When our financial picture looks bleak, we may be tempted to bury our head in the sand and refuse to face reality because it seems so frightening. Unfortunately this fear can cause us to react in unproductive ways, like stuffing overdue bills into a drawer because we can't pay them, or avoiding balancing our checkbook because we're afraid to see the balance.

Eventually we learn that avoidance only makes negative conditions worse. If we instead make a commitment to face our current situation, we often realize that it isn't as bad as we feared. Taking it a step further, we can also decide to get organized and create a plan for improvement in the future – and that is often enough to make us feel empowered. Taking just one step in faith is often enough to get the ball rolling in a more positive direction.

Affirmation:

Doing what I can do today is enough.

Day 2

If you can imagine it, you can achieve it. If you can dream it, you can become it.

- William Arthur Ward

Are your financial goals big enough to keep you feeling motivated? Many times we set smaller goals because we believe they are all we can handle, but those smaller goals are rarely exciting enough to ignite our passion and determination. As a result, we take little pleasure from achieving these goals – or even give up on them because they couldn't hold our interest long enough to see them through to the end.

Rather than settling for what we think we can achieve, we should learn to expand our minds as William Arthur Ward suggests above. A good way to start is by asking ourselves, "What is the biggest vision I can conceive for my financial future?" then writing it down in full detail. Doing this automatically inspires our subconscious mind to begin formulating a plan for the fulfillment of our vision – often in surprising and wonderful ways.

Affirmation:

Today I dare to dream bigger than I ever have.

Day 3

Think big and kick ass.

- Donald Trump

Many of us have a chronic habit of thinking small and limiting ourselves at every turn. We can easily come up with a thousand reasons why we can't do something, why we can't become successful like so-and-so, and why we'll probably never achieve what we really want so we may as well settle for what we can get.

What if we stopped all the self-limiting jargon and began to stretch our minds to what is really possible? What if we dared to dream bigger and set goals that to other people would seem impossible? The funny thing about mind-set is that it usually determines our destination. Dream big, win big; limit ourselves, get limited results. It really is up to us what we achieve, based on our perception of whether or not it is possible.

Affirmation:

I am capable of so much more than I can imagine.

Day 4

More gold has been mined from the thoughts of men than has been taken from the earth.

- Napoleon Hill

Regardless how hopeless our present circumstances may seem, we must remember that as long as we have the ability to think, we have all the power we need to improve our lives. This can be difficult to remember when we feel stuck in situations that we can't control, but if nothing else we do have the power to control the way we perceive what is happening around us.

Deliberately controlling our thoughts gives us the power to dream of a better future, create plans to begin moving toward that future – and most importantly, to turn our attention away from things that make us feel disempowered and frightened. Very often just taking control of our thoughts like this is enough to trigger positive change and attract better circumstances.

Affirmation:

Today I deliberately choose to think empowering thoughts.

Day 5

You are the most powerful magnet in the universe! You contain a magnetic power within you that is more powerful than anything in this world, and this unfathomable magnetic power is emitted through your thoughts.

- Rhonda Byrne

These powerful words by Rhonda Byrne remind us that we are anything but helpless victims of a harsh universe. The problem is that we often can't see any way we could have attracted something unpleasant into our lives. Financial hardship, job loss, recession; who in their right mind would want to attract these things?

Most often we aren't even consciously focusing on these things so they seem like complete surprises, but what is actually happening is that we are forgetting to focus on the opposite conditions we DO want to create. Learning to control and direct our thoughts toward better circumstances can go a long way in minimizing unpleasant surprises.

Affirmation:

My thoughts are constantly broadcasting my preferences.

Day 6

If opportunity doesn't knock, build a door.

- Milton Berle

Very often in life we find ourselves sitting and waiting for opportunities to fall into our lap – and unfortunately, doing so often means we will be waiting for a long time. We can benefit by remembering that opportunities can be created simply by taking bold action toward something we want. When we put ourselves out there in the world, we end up meeting people who can help make things happen for us, or otherwise find ourselves in the "right place at the right time."

While seemingly random opportunities can appear in our lives, we are much more likely to achieve success if we don't wait idly for them to arrive. The truth is that we already have everything we need to create our success, and chance opportunities simply complement that existing potential. In fact, what we need more than opportunities is the belief that we can create opportunities whenever we like.

Affirmation:

I create opportunities by taking action.

Day 7

Get up, stand up! Get up for your life!

- Bob Marley

Long-standing financial struggle can often spark an underlying belief that we don't deserve more than we currently have, as well as convince us that it is impossible to improve our circumstances. Over time hopelessness, defeat and resignation become our dominant thoughts and our dreams of success and abundance slowly start to fade from our minds.

Bob Marley offers a powerful reminder that it is up to us to stand up and fight for what we want, whether it be more money, freedom, opportunities, or simply happiness. The most important parts of taking a stand are to develop an unwavering belief that we deserve better and set forth a strong intention to have it. Interestingly, just the act of doing these simple things is often what begins drawing more opportunities for change into our lives.

Affirmation:

I deserve better and I choose to do better now.

Day 8

Do what you can with what you have, where you are.

- Theodore Roosevelt

Too often we hold back on pursuing our dreams because we can't figure out how the whole process will unfold. We know where we want to end up but can't see the journey fully so we hang back and do nothing, allowing anxiety to erode our confidence and motivation.

Refusing to take any action at all just because some parts of the plan are unclear is like refusing to hike along a beautiful forest trail because we can't see what lies around the next bend. We think we are wisely avoiding pitfalls – but all we're really doing is denying ourselves the joy of discovery. If we instead just relax and enjoy moving forward, we usually discover that the pathway before us continues to get clearer with every step we take.

Affirmation:

Everything is easier if I take one step at a time.

Day 9

Remember, no more effort is required in order to aim high in life, to demand abundance and prosperity, than is required to accept misery and poverty.

– Napoleon Hill

How easy it is to forget that we have a choice in the circumstances we experience each day. Our physical surroundings may appear to be solid and unchangeable - but once we begin exploring the true power of our thoughts we quickly realize that a shift in mind-set is often enough to transform even the most difficult situations.

Napoleon Hill is right when he reminds us that the level of effort is the same no matter what we choose to believe and see in our lives. We can choose to see ourselves as financially challenged or growing more in abundance every day. We can choose to believe that we are capable of achieving amazing things; or that we are stuck right where we are. The effort we invest in these alternate realities is the same – just the outcome is different.

Affirmation:

I invest my energy into wealth and success.

Day 10

Wherever you see a successful business, someone once made a courageous decision.

- Peter Drucker

Some of us have learned to avoid taking risks because we fear possible negative consequences, but we often fail to see that risks can be opportunities in disguise. If we were to ask a group of highly successful people how they became successful, many of them would likely mention taking a chance against all odds or otherwise moving beyond their comfort zones. In other words, they had to be courageous.

The greatest thing about courage is that it does not require an absence of fear – but rather the determination to move forward in spite of uncertainty. That means that each and every one of us can be courageous whenever we want to. We don't have to wait until we are rich, successful, and powerful before courageously going after what we want. In fact, without courage it would be virtually impossible to achieve those things anyway. Courage must come first.

Affirmation:

I choose to be courageous in everything I do.

Day 11

Another day can equal another chance.

- Donald Trump

Somewhere along the way many of us ended up believing that "failure" is a dead-end. Perhaps we tried to achieve something (or many different things) and it didn't work out the way we planned so we drew the conclusion that nothing ever will work out for us. We forget that every so-called "failure" actually teaches us a lot about ourselves and helps us better clarify our vision of success.

No matter how many times we have failed in the past, it is never too late to try again. Each and every day we have the opportunity to wipe the slate clean and conceive new dreams, new goals, new beliefs about who we are and what we can achieve. We truly have nothing to lose if we keep taking the chances that each new day brings.

Affirmation:

I am starting anew right now.

Day 12

A journey of a thousand miles must begin with a single step.

- Chinese proverb

The bigger a dream is, the more likely it is to overwhelm us – sometimes to the point that we don't do anything because we don't know if we'll be able to finish what we started. However, if we can push ourselves to take just one step forward, we usually realize that it wasn't as difficult as we feared it would be. Our confidence begins to grow and we find we are able to take another step, and then another.

Before long we are moving steadily forward, making progress, building momentum, and wondering why we ever hesitated in the first place. We need to remind ourselves that the first step is usually the hardest, but if we refuse to be held back by fear or doubt we make the entire journey smoother and much more enjoyable.

Affirmation:

Every step I take is easier than the last.

Day 13

A purpose is the eternal condition of success.

- Theodore T. Munger

When in the midst of financial struggle it is natural to think that the obvious solution is the acquisition of more money. We focus intently on the actions we can take to earn more money or attract better opportunities, all the while forgetting that there is another way.

Observing some of the wealthiest people on the planet, we see that many of them obtained their wealth by focusing not on how to increase their bottom line but on what they could offer to others. They tapped into their creativity, conceived a purpose to direct their actions, then contributed as much value to society as they could - and wealth was automatically drawn to them. From these examples we learn that wealth is more meaningful when it is the result of fulfilling an inner purpose.

Affirmation:

I am richly compensated for fulfilling my purpose.

Day 14

All it takes is a dream, a team, and a theme to create a stream of perpetual income.

- Mark Victor Hansen & Robert G. Allen

Most of us are good at dreaming; we have lofty visions of what we would like our lives to be like, how much money we would like to have, and the many goals we would like to achieve in our lifetime. We often forget, however, that we don't have to do it all on our own. Aligning our vision with those of likeminded people can magnify our own vision and allow us to achieve even greater levels of success than we could by flying solo.

Likewise, creating a "theme" for our life – something we stand for, fight for, or believe deeply in – can have the same magnifying effect on our actions because we are always keenly aware that our efforts benefit many other people, not just ourselves. True success is about having a purpose, aligning with others to work together, and of course being willing to stretch our mind about what is possible for all of us.

Affirmation:

As I open my mind and heart, I attract perfect partnerships.

Day 15

The mightiest works have been accomplished by men who have kept their ability to dream great dreams.

- Walter Bowie

Imagine if Thomas Edison had given up after a few attempts to create the electric light bulb, or if the great Egyptian pyramids were never built because people of that time decided the stones were just too heavy to move. When we look at great achievers from past generations, we might think that those people had something we don't have. We assume they must have been more talented, or stronger, more focused, or otherwise had better opportunities than we have today.

The truth is that we are no different than they were. In fact, today we have far more resources and opportunities at our fingertips than they ever did. What many of us lack is not talent, skill or opportunity, but tenacity. We haven't learned how to look beyond obstacles and focus on the solutions, how to ask ourselves "what now" instead of "why not?" If we simply refused to let our dreams die as Walter Bowie suggests, we might find ourselves indeed creating "mighty works" like our forebears.

Affirmation:

No obstacle can be so big that it tempts me to give up.

Day 16

Only those who dare to fail greatly, can ever achieve greatly.

- Robert F. Kennedy

Not many of us like the idea of failure, and it's not too hard to figure out why. There are few experiences that cause such intense feelings of disappointment, discouragement and frustration as working toward a goal and feeling like you aren't getting anywhere. However, even worse that the initial letdown is what failure can do to us long-term if we allow it: erode our belief in our own ability to succeed and create a perception of powerlessness in virtually every area of our lives.

It is important to understand that these despondent feelings have nothing to do with failure itself but rather our perception of the failure. We attach all kinds of meanings to our inability to achieve a goal, like thinking we must be destined to a lifetime of poverty and struggle, or that we are stuck in mediocrity, that we will never be successful and so on. Rather than drawing such conclusions, we can learn to recognize that every perceived failure is merely a stepping stone along the path to success. Failure is a necessary part of learning and growing – not something to be ashamed of.

Affirmation:

I turn failures into life lessons.

Day 17

*Twenty years from now you will be more
disappointed by the things that you didn't do than
by the ones you did do. So throw off the bowlines.
Sail away from the safe harbor. Catch the trade
winds in your sales. Explore, dream, discover.*

- Mark Twain

This famous quote by Mark Twain reminds us that
we have little to lose by acting boldly in every area
of our lives, and this is especially true when it
comes to success and wealth. While a
conservative approach may feel safer, it can also
be quite restrictive and limiting. This becomes a
problem because allowing fear to restrict our
actions creates another unpleasant consequence -
little or no results from our efforts.

If we instead learn how to take bigger – yet
calculated – risks, we realize that boldness often
pays off much more quickly than caution does.
Obviously, there is a difference between boldness
and recklessness. Our inner guidance can always
help us to temper courage with patience and
determination with clarity, which creates the perfect
environment for the creation of our success.

Affirmation:

I trust myself to know the right actions to take.

Day 18

The shortest and best way to make your fortune is to let people see clearly that it is in their best interest to promote yours.

- Jean De La Bruyere

This quote by Jean De La Bruyere is a powerful reminder that people are more apt to help us in our endeavors if they stand to gain something for their efforts. Rather than seeing this as an example of selfishness, we can learn to use it to our advantage by building a network of people who benefit from our efforts as we also benefit from theirs.

This may involve forming mutually beneficial partnerships, sharing referrals, or even doing our part to help make someone else successful before we ourselves begin to enjoy success. When we step back to look at the big picture and see that there are endless ways to help others and ourselves at the same time, everyone wins.

Affirmation:

I easily receive ideas that can help others and myself.

Day 19

No mistake or failure is as bad as to stop and not try again.

- John Wanamaker

Have you ever wondered how close you may have been to achieving success right before you gave up? It has been said that the tougher the going gets, the closer you are to a breakthrough. Granted it doesn't usually feel that way, but a belief in this possibility is what separates those who are truly determined to achieve success from those who don't yet have what it takes.

One of the most powerful lessons we can learn in life is stated beautifully by John Wanamaker when he reminds us that there truly is no failure unless we stop trying. While in the midst of struggle, it seems like there is no other option but to admit defeat and give up – but that is never a solution, only a temporary reprieve. By instead pushing through the obstacles we are virtually guaranteed to achieve a certain measure of success.

Affirmation:

I can't fail if I don't give up.

Day 20

You don't get to choose how you're going to die, or when. You can only decide how you're going to live. Now!

- John Baez

How much time do we spend worrying about tomorrow? In fact, we worry about so many things that are out of our control – the world economy, who is losing money, who has much more than they need or deserve . . . and so much more. Sadly, as we focus so much of our time and energy on these situations we can't control, we end up missing out on the present moment.

There is great power in staying focused on the present moment – in fact, when it comes right down to it the present moment is all we have. When we switch our focus to empowering ourselves right now, in this moment, we automatically begin creating a better, more prosperous future for ourselves and others. Even better, simply by removing our focus from worrisome topics, our present moment begins to look a lot brighter too.

Affirmation:

I choose to focus on wealth and abundance for all.

Day 21

Control your thinking, and you control your results.

- Mark Victor Hansen & Robert G. Allen

Have you ever allowed worry to cloud your thinking and affect your results? The irony is that we usually worry because we think it will help us avoid disaster – but all it really does is contribute more energy to the very things we are worrying about; and it doesn't end there, either.

Worrisome thoughts also have a large impact on the actions we take – or don't take – on a daily basis. In this context, we see clearly that negative thoughts are destructive on many levels. Once we have begun to realize the true power of our thoughts, we have a responsibility to use them wisely by consciously choosing to focus on abundance, hold positive expectations, and demand the success we deserve.

Affirmation:

I focus only on what I want to experience.

Day 22

Ain't no chances if you don't take it.

- Guy Clark

Have you ever been too frightened to grab hold of an opportunity that was presented to you? Maybe you worried that it must be "too good to be true" so you didn't trust it. Perhaps someone close to you warned that you weren't capable of achieving such a thing, so it would be better not to try at all.

Whatever way it played out, you can probably still feel a sense of disappointment about not taking the chance when you had the opportunity. While it may be too late to take advantage of the chances you left in the past, there is nothing stopping you from making a promise to yourself right now that you will grab hold of present and future opportunities without a second of hesitation.

Affirmation:

As I take advantage of one opportunity, many more rush in.

Day 23

No man becomes rich unless he enriches others.

- Andrew Carnegie

This quote by Andrew Carnegie brilliantly sums up the "golden rule" of doing unto others as you would have done unto you. That means much more than treating people kindly – it's really about the contribution you make to the world, and the corresponding compensation that the universe returns back to you.

A good shortcut to true wealth is to figure out a way to make a meaningful contribution to as many people as you can. What do you have to offer the world? What makes you unique? What talents or gifts can you use to create something of value that would help others? When the answers to these questions have come clear in your mind, you have an obvious path to wealth.

Affirmation:

I believe I can make a powerful positive difference in the world.

Day 24

You will never leave where you are until you decide where you'd rather be.

- Dexter Yager

Dexter Yager's words aptly convey the power of focus when it comes to the quality of our lives. Many of us start with a dream to create something better, but are often stumped when it comes to figuring out exactly what that something is. Even worse, we spend the majority of our time focusing on our problems, challenges, and disappointments.

Is it any wonder that nothing changes in our surroundings? Transforming our lives requires three things: first, decide where we'd rather be – in full detail. Second, create a plan to get there. And third, begin focusing most of our attention on that destination, not merely fantasizing about it but also adopting the thoughts, beliefs and actions of a person who is determined to have it.

Affirmation:

In my mind I am already wealthy and successful.

Day 25

Minds are like parachutes. They only function when they are open.

- Sir James Dewar

The problem many of us have is not that we are not capable of achieving great wealth and success – but that we have closed our minds to the many great ideas that could put us on the path to such an outcome. Have you ever gotten a great idea that caused your heart to beat faster and you began daydreaming about how awesome it would be to accomplish such a thing?

Then most likely the doubt and disbelief crept in. You may have thought, "I don't have the money or knowledge to do that; no one would take me seriously," and so on. Doubt and disbelief are symptoms of a closed mind – and wealth and success cannot come from that type of mind-set. Instead, open your mind; let the ideas flow in, and then do whatever you can to follow through on them and see where they might lead.

Affirmation:

Today I open my mind to inspiration.

Day 26

If you're thinking of debt, that's what you're going to attract.

- Bob Proctor

We often take a "destructive" approach in improving our lives by trying to blast the negative stuff out of our consciousness - as if hating something intently enough could remove it permanently. However, as Bob Proctor so eloquently states, the more we focus on the negative the more we are going to keep perpetuating it in our lives.

One of the most powerful techniques we can learn is the ability to switch the angle of our focus. Rather than trying to avoid focusing on the negative stuff, we can learn to see it in a different light - for example, imagining ourselves as being debt-free, rather than resisting the feeling of being in debt. It seems like such a small shift, but it can make all the difference in the world.

Affirmation:

Every negative situation has a more positive angle.

Day 27

Do just once what others say you can't do, and you will never pay attention to their limitations again.

- James R. Cook

Has anyone ever talked you out of doing something you wanted to do? Perhaps a parent or teacher tried to help you "face reality" when you excitedly shared your dream of becoming an astronaut; or a friend scoffed when you told him you wanted to build a multi-billion dollar corporation someday.

Believe it or not, the problem isn't that the people around you sometimes appear to be unsupportive; the problem is that they are expressing their belief in limits – and you have willingly adopted those limitations as your own. Turning this around is a simple matter of doing what your heart is leading you to do anyway. Limits have a way of dissolving after you push through them.

Affirmation:

Limits do not exist in my world.

Day 28

All my life I've wanted to be someone; I guess I should have been more specific.

- Jane Wagner/Lily Tomlin

This humorous quote reminds us that we need to be specific when we think about the things we want. It is not enough to wish for wealth, success, and happiness because those things will look different to everyone who imagines them. If we instead take some time to clarify our own definitions of wealth, success, and happiness, we stand a much better chance of creating them.

At the same time, it is also important to avoid getting too attached to the way these things come into our lives. Though we may think we always know what is best for us, sometimes the universe has even better ideas that include outcomes we never could have imagined – but are thrilled to see when they arrive.

Affirmation:

The universe constantly leads me to my highest good.

Day 29

I'm a millionaire, I'm a multi-millionaire. I'm filthy
rich. You know why I'm a multi-millionaire? 'Cause
multi-millions like what I do.

- Michael Moore

Michael Moore's powerful words remind us that our
success depends on the number of lives we are
able to enhance. Touching millions of lives may
seem like an intimidating prospect, but we must
remember that it does not have to be accomplished
in one day.

Imagine instead touching a handful of lives every
day for the rest of your life, or creating something
wonderful that begins to take on a life of its own
and spread around the world, inspiring and
empowering millions of people to do even more
good in the world. These possibilities and more are
highly probable if you simply do what you love and
reach out as best you can.

Affirmation:

Passion multiplies my results.

Day 30

If you do the right job then money will come to you. Because people who need you will request, will ask for you, will attract you, and will be willing to pay you for your services.

- Jose Silva

This quote is a great example of how doing work we love can create a ripple effect and attract the very things we need in order to become more and more successful. What Jose Silva doesn't mention, however, is the importance of infusing everything we do with excellence.

Imagine a brilliant surgeon who shows up late to work each day and does sloppy work. Would his patients be pleased with his services? Would they refer their friends to see him? Probably not. Doing the right job is important – but even more important is HOW you do it. Putting your heart and soul into everything you do cannot help but attract amazing things back to you.

Affirmation:

I give my absolute best to everything I do.

Day 31

Money never starts an idea. It is always the idea that starts the money.

- Owen Laughlin

As much as we would like to remove all difficult or troublesome circumstances from our lives, we must remember that these are some of the most fertile periods we will ever experience. It is during moments of intense fear or frustration that we often receive the best ideas for creating much more beneficial circumstances.

To better demonstrate this concept, ask yourself this: If you already had everything you wanted and tons of money in the bank, how motivated would you be to improve your life or create a positive difference in the world? For most of us, the answer would be, "Not very motivated." The truth is, we need challenges to stimulate our minds, to push us to higher and higher levels of achievement, and that is when true wealth begins to flow in.

Affirmation:

I am rich with motivating ideas.

Day 32

*A pessimist sees the difficulty in every opportunity;
an optimist sees the opportunity in every difficulty.*

- Sir Winston Churchill

The most defining moments of our lives happen when we encounter obstacles. Many of us have gotten used to seeing obstacles as uncontrollable stopping points. We throw our hands up and declare, "I can't do it," or "It's just not meant to be." However, Winston Churchill shares a glimpse of another possibility: learning to find the opportunity in every difficulty.

All it takes to do so is a slight shift in attitude. Rather than concluding that obstacles mean imminent failure, we can decide that they present a chance to be a bit more creative by asking, "What can I learn from this situation?" Doing this immediately moves you back into the driver's seat. And though uttering this question may not make our obstacles disappear immediately, we at least feel more empowered to find a way to get around them.

Affirmation:

I choose to see opportunities everywhere.

Day 33

Should you find yourself in a chronically leaking boat, energy devoted to changing vessels is likely to be more productive than energy devoted to patching leaks.

- Warren Buffet

It can be difficult to know whether a goal is truly unrealistic and futile, or if we simply haven't given it enough effort and should push forward until we make progress. This quote by Warren Buffet is illuminating because of one word: "chronically".

A "chronically leaking boat" could be defined as one that is beyond repair. The only way to salvage something that is truly falling apart is to rebuild it from scratch. If we apply this concept to our goals and dreams, we are able to see at a glance whether we should scrap our idea and start again, or simply patch the small leaks and keep rowing toward shore.

Affirmation:

Clarity guides my every move.

Day 34

Think and grow rich.

- Napoleon Hill

As much as we love the idea of using our thoughts to create our lives, most of us are aware that it takes a little bit more than merely thinking about wealth in order to manifest it. Certainly, aligning our thoughts with wealth is a powerful first step, but there must also be an intention to be wealthy, and an unwavering belief that we can indeed be wealthy.

Finally, we must be willing to believe that we deserve to be wealthy. Many of us forget this last part and instead spend hours visualizing, taking action, hoping and praying for our circumstances to improve – and all the while our subconscious mind is simply blocking the very thing we want because we feel unworthy of having it.

Affirmation:

I deserve wealth just as much as those who already have it.

Day 35

Everything that can be invented has been invented.

- Charles H. Duell, Commissioner, U.S. Office of Patents, 1899

Have you ever had a great idea and then immediately felt like you would just be mimicking people who have already accomplished similar works? This quote by Charles H. Duell is eye-opening when you consider just how many wonderful things have been invented since he uttered these words.

Not only are there endless new ideas waiting to be conceived by all of us, it is also possible to keep improving upon and expanding the things that already exist in our world. The greatest part about this is that anything YOU create will have your own energy woven through it, and it would be completely unique from the same thing created by someone else.

Affirmation:

My creations are as unique as I am.

Day 36

Whenever you find you are on the side of the majority, it is time to pause and reflect.

- Mark Twain

Have you ever heard it said that progressive thinkers are always ahead of their time? Mark Twain's words here are in perfect alignment with that concept. In our younger years most of us expend a fair amount of energy trying to fit in with our peers, but as we get older we begin to see the benefits of thinking for ourselves, even if it makes us seem different than the majority.

Being different is a good thing because it shows that we are not simply adopting other people's beliefs and limitations for ourselves. We are creating the life that is best for us, regardless of what others may think about it. While this may not always be a comfortable position to be in, it is infinitely more comfortable than hiding our light under a bushel and denying our true nature.

Affirmation:

It is okay to think for myself.

Day 37

A cynic is a man who knows the price of everything, and the value of nothing.

- Oscar Wilde

A strong focus on wealth accumulation can often cause us to lose sight of the things that really matter in life. It is certainly natural and understandable to have a strong desire to create a more stable financial picture – and never is this more urgent than when we are in the midst of financial struggle. However, the more we remove our focus from what we already have and place it on what we are trying to gain, the less wealthy we feel.

If we instead make it a habit to appreciate what we already have while also working to create more things to appreciate, we can literally have the best of both worlds. Believe it or not, there are people who have far more money than they will ever need but feel like the poorest people on the planet. Focusing on our existing blessings will always help us avoid that trap.

Affirmation:

I am already wealthy in so many ways.

Day 38

To attract money, you must focus on wealth. It is impossible to bring more money into your life when you are noticing you do not have enough, because that means you are thinking thoughts that you do not have enough.

- Rhonda Byrne

This quote by Rhonda Byrne seems simple enough in theory, but many of us struggle to put it into action. Let's face it; it is extremely hard NOT to focus on lack when it is constantly staring us in the face. When there is nothing we can physically do to improve our circumstances, our natural reaction is to worry.

The problem is that doing this keeps sending the same "signal" to the universe, conveying the message that we are stuck in financial lack – and we will simply keep repeating the same cycle of lack over and over again. As difficult as it may seem, we must find a way to focus on the good feelings that wealth inspires, even if we can only do it by pretending right now.

Affirmation:

I can create any reality I want in my mind.

Day 39

The true measure of a man is how he treats someone who can do him absolutely no good.

- Samuel Johnson

Have you ever noticed that some wealthy and successful people are rude to the people who serve them? For example, a wealthy businessman who barks orders at his assistant, or insults a waitress in a restaurant because his soup is cold. If these examples trigger a wave of disgust in you, you may want to consider whether part of you could be resisting wealth because you fear becoming rude and uncaring.

Logically you may know that rudeness has nothing to do with having money, but deep down inside you may still be operating from the belief that having money is somehow bad or will turn you into a bad person. Exploring this possibility can be incredibly helpful because you are able to consciously form beliefs that will support you in your intention to be wealthy and successful.

Affirmation:

I can choose to be kind no matter how much money I have.

Day 40

When your desires are strong enough you will appear to possess superhuman powers to achieve.

- Napoleon Hill

When we look back at past goals we set and never achieved, it is often clear that we made poor progress because we didn't care enough to put forth a strong intensity of effort. Conversely, there may have been things we wanted so desperately that we did whatever it took to make them happen. Failure was simply not an option with those goals.

Which category do your current goals and aspirations fall into? Are you truly willing to do whatever it takes to achieve them, or do you often find yourself losing determination or procrastinating when it comes time to work on them? If it's the latter, you may want to spend some time tweaking your goal until it becomes so important that you can't NOT achieve it.

Affirmation:

Anything is possible if I want it badly enough.

Day 41

You can only become truly accomplished at something you love. Don't make money your goal. Instead, pursue the things you love doing, and then do them so well that people can't take their eyes off you.

- Maya Angelou

These wise words from Maya Angelou make it clear that we cannot become wildly successful at something we don't enjoy. Yet many of us start out trying to do just that. We see a person who is successful at a specific activity and we think that we could attain success too if we just follow their example. Eventually we realize that success has nothing to do with the activity, but has everything to do with the person who is performing the activity.

Another challenge is that many of us have no idea what we love to do – or how to earn money doing it even if we do have an idea. This is where self-reflection can be a useful tool, because deep inside we truly do know the answers to both of these questions. We simply have to ask and listen for the guidance that inevitably follows.

Affirmation:

The singing of my heart is a beacon that shows me the way to success.

Day 42

Formal education will make you a living; self-education will make you a fortune.

 - Jim Rohn

We often turn over much of our power to institutions and programs and that dispense knowledge and forget that we ourselves can be our greatest teachers. Formal education is certainly a valuable and positive way to enhance our opportunities in life, but it often falls short by failing to emphasize the importance of thinking for ourselves and expanding our education continuously.

Jim Rohn reminds us that self-education can be more lucrative than limiting ourselves to what others teach us. If we make an effort to learn from every experience, we will embark on a journey of consistent inner growth and evolvement that will pay off forever. Not only will we find it easier to make more money, we will expand and enrich every aspect of our lives.

Affirmation:

I am always growing in wisdom and mastery.

Day 43

What we really want to do is what we are really meant to do. When we do what we are meant to do, money comes to us, doors open for us, we feel useful, and the work we do feels like play to us.

- Julia Cameron

Have you ever worried that you couldn't figure out what you were meant to do while you were here? Have you ever felt like you were supposed to be doing something else but weren't sure what it was? Some people spend years agonizing over these questions, but in fact the solution is very simple: do what you really want to do.

As Julia Cameron so vividly describes, we are all meant to do what we really want to do in life. That means that the very things that make you feel happy and alive while you do them are the things you are meant to share with the world. Discovering the right vehicle for doing so may take a little more time and effort, but just having the first part figured out is a great first step.

Affirmation:

I follow my passions and find success.

Day 44

If you keep doing what you have always done, you'll keep getting what you've always got.

- Jim Rohn

Have you ever noticed that you tend to get into "ruts" much of the time? These ruts can appear in your day to day activities, like always taking the same route to work, eating the same meals week after week; or even setting the same goals every year – and failing to achieve those same goals every year.

Amazing things can happen when you decide to shake up your life and do something different. Try wearing a daring new outfit or ordering an exotic dish in a restaurant. Create a new, exciting spin on those goals and take bold action on them immediately. Just being willing to try something new will usually empower you to blaze new trails in every area of your life.

Affirmation:

I am willing to step out of my comfort zones.

Day 45

Money is only a tool. It will take you wherever you wish, but it will not replace you as the driver.

- Ayn Rand

What a great reminder that money is not the be all and end all in our lives! On some level we already know that money isn't good or bad. We know that it can't buy happiness, or love, or peace. But we still often believe that having more money would make us feel better. We envision ourselves feeling more confident, joyful, purposeful, and fulfilled. The truth is that money cannot provide any of those things.

Certainly having enough money allows us create a comfortable, stable and secure lifestyle, but it cannot change anything unless we decide to change it. Money is just a tool that gives us more options, nothing more. Just as a hammer or screwdriver can't build a house, money cannot create our lives; that is up to us to do.

Affirmation:

I appreciate all tools for making my life easier.

Day 46

Money will buy you a fine dog, but only love can make it wag its tail.

- Richard Friedman

Richard Friedman offers a great insight with this quote about the power of love and happiness. Have you ever spent time fantasizing about the wonderful things you would buy if you could afford anything you wanted? Do you imagine a beautiful home, luxury car, exotic vacation, or expensive artwork?

These things and more can be satisfying, but it's important to look beyond the acquisition of them and determine the qualities they would contribute to your life. An expensive painting can be a worthwhile investment, but would it bring you joy to gaze upon it? True wealth is not about buying things because you can, but rather buying them because they add something wonderful to your life.

Affirmation:

I surround myself with love and beauty.

Day 47

To get rich never risk your health. For it is the truth that health is the wealth of wealth.

- Richard Baker

Sometimes when we want a particular outcome very badly but don't see results quickly enough, we may be tempted to work extra hard and sacrifice more important things in order to obtain it. The problem with this is that there are always consequences that come with sacrifices. Poor health, fractured relationships, and chronic stress are just a few of the negative consequences of pushing too hard.

We would do well to remember that trying to force something to happen before its time is a futile undertaking. Either it won't turn out the way we hoped, or we will end up hurting ourselves and others in the process. Patience and persistence will go a long way in attracting success; and it will happen in a smooth and natural way.

Affirmation:

I care for myself as much as I care for my goals.

Day 48

Money is usually attracted, not pursued.

- Jim Rohn

Have you ever noticed that the harder you pursue an elusive quality, the faster it seems to move away from you? Constantly chasing money will almost certainly create more and more situations where you must keep chasing money. Likewise if you are chasing love, security, happiness or anything else.

A much better approach is to make friends with this elusive quality you want. Woo it, romance it, entice it to want to be with you. How exactly do you do this? Simply by thinking positively about having it and taking deliberate actions that will allow it to flow forth. The physical part in each case isn't much different – it's just the attitudes that are miles apart.

Affirmation:

Money loves people who feel wealthy.

Day 49

By changing your thoughts it's possible to begin attracting mountains of money, riches, wealth and prosperity into your life.

- Sandy Forster

If you had to determine which of your consistent thoughts may be preventing you from achieving the level of wealth and success you desire, what do you think those thoughts would be? You are likely aware that negative thoughts in general are harmful because they continue to attract more negative circumstances into your life.

For example, constant worry, fear, anxiety and stress are counterproductive. However, there are other thoughts that can be equally damaging, like envy, bitterness, futility, frustration, doubt, and anger. If you tend to focus on any of these frequently, try turning these negative thoughts into more positive, loving thoughts and watch how your experiences begin to transform too.

Affirmation:

Everything I experience starts with my thoughts.

Day 50

God does not want us to do extraordinary things: He wants us to do ordinary things extraordinarily well.

- Bishop Gore

Have you ever held back on a goal or dream because you felt it was beyond your ability to achieve it? Bishop Gore's words are a great reminder that we do not have to attempt to do "extraordinary" things – most of which we doubt we could achieve anyway.

Instead, we simply need to do ordinary things extraordinarily well – which means giving them our full effort and doing them over and over again until we have mastered them. Persistence, practice and patience can be even more potent than natural skill or talent; enabling us to keep moving forward until we have successfully achieved our goal.

Affirmation:

I can become great at anything if I do it enough times.

Day 51

Only a fool holds out for the top dollar.

- Joseph P. Kennedy

Sometimes we create obstacles for ourselves because we resist the necessity of starting where we are and working our way up the ladder to bigger and better things. While it is natural to want to make the most progress possible in a short amount of time, holding back until that "perfect" opportunity arrives can be counterproductive.

We can often make much faster progress if we just roll up our sleeves and make the best of where we are right now, while also striving to reach greater levels of success as we go. Not only does immediate action begin drawing better opportunities into our lives, we end up feeling better about our current circumstances because we are taking a proactive role in creating our success.

Affirmation:

No matter where I start, I am always looking forward.

Day 52

Everything comes too late for those who only wait.

- Elbert Hubbard

Are you waiting for your life circumstances to improve in some way before you begin pursuing your goals in earnest? Perhaps you feel that your family needs you too much right now so you can't spare enough time for yourself; or your job places too many demands on your time and energy, or conditions otherwise seem less than optimal.

There are endless reasons you can talk yourself out of moving forward, but the truth remains that there will never be a perfect time to go after what you want. There will always be other demands on your time, energy, and resources. There will always be fears and excuses lurking in the back of your mind. The question is whether you want to allow them to hold you back any longer.

Affirmation:

Now is the perfect time to begin moving forward on my dreams.

Day 53

Obstacles are the scary things you see when you take your eyes off your goals.

- Russ Whitney

Russ Whitney's creative quote aptly sums up what happens to most of us when we encounter obstacles: we stop focusing on where we want to end up and start focusing more on the things that are preventing us from getting there. While obstacles can be frustrating for sure, dwelling on them is one sure way to fail every time.

By focusing so much of our attention and energy on obstacles, we end up creating more stress for ourselves and further clouding our ability to think clearly. If we instead learn to see obstacles as necessary but manageable inconveniences, we will be able to keep our eyes squarely on our destination and keep moving steadily forward.

Affirmation:

I focus all of my energy on making steady progress.

Day 54

When you change your thinking, you change your beliefs; When you change your beliefs, you change your expectations; When you change your expectations, you change your attitude; When you change your attitude, you change your behavior; When you change your behavior, you change your performance; When you change your performance, you change your life!

- Dr. Walter Doyle Staples

It is easy to get caught up in the perception that improving our lives is a daunting task until we remember that there is a very clear progression of smaller changes that inevitably lead us in the direction we want to go. Dr. Walter Doyle Staples' words remind us that just the simple act of choosing better thoughts can trigger a landslide of positive change.

Applying this concept to our financial condition is no different. Think thoughts of abundance and ease rather than struggle and lack; believe abundance is already ours; expect more abundance to keep showing up; feel more abundant as a result; take action to bring more abundance into our lives – and abundance is magnetically drawn to us.

Affirmation:

I am always in control of what I choose to think.

Day 55

Chance favors the prepared mind.

- Louis Pasteur

We tend to think of chance as being completely random but Louis Pasteur reminds us that preparation will usually attract more opportunities than we would receive by simply waiting for something to happen. How can we prepare our minds for success and wealth?

By believing we deserve to be successful and wealthy; by making room in our lives for the better circumstances we seek; and by clearing our environment (both mental and physical) of negativity. In other words, we need to align ourselves on all levels with wealth and success long before it arrives on our doorstep.

Affirmation:

I am prepared to receive abundance now.

Day 56

The harder you work, the harder it is to surrender.

- Vince Lombardi

Vince Lombardi's wise words share a powerful insight about one of the great secrets of success: the more time and energy we invest into our goals, the less likely we are to give up on them. When it comes to your financial goals, consider how much time and energy you have poured into creating a better life for yourself and your family.

Have you done everything you could do up to this point in time? Could you be more focused or committed to your goals? Do you need to take your efforts to the next level? Whatever you have done so far, multiply your efforts times ten – and make the prospect of quitting extremely uncomfortable.

Affirmation:

I stand to gain much more by forging ahead.

Day 57

What you think of me is none of my business. What is most important is what I think about myself.

- Robert Kiyosaki

Do you ever avoid taking action on something because you are afraid of what other people would think about it (or what they would think about you for doing it)? Most often these fears are based on prior experiences when you may have been ridiculed, scolded, or rejected for something you did long ago.

A good way to overcome these limiting thoughts is to remember that other people will usually see you as a reflection of the way you see yourself. Believing in yourself and feeling confident about the things you do will often trigger like responses from others - and the opinions of those who feel differently are literally "none of your business". All that matters is how you feel about yourself.

Affirmation:

I am proud of myself for everything I do.

Day 58

Opportunities are usually disguised as hard work, so most people don't recognize them.

- Ann Landers

Have you gotten into the habit of always seeking the "easy way" to achieve your goals? More often than not, the easy way carries a hefty price. Either you have to sacrifice portions of your dream that cannot be accomplished in a fast and easy way, or you notice with disappointment that the outcome isn't as satisfying as you hoped.

Rather than trying to avoid hard work, it may be helpful to differentiate between hard work and struggle. More often than not we are not averse to working hard; we simply don't want to struggle needlessly. With a little preparation, organization and patience, we can accomplish much without the need to struggle and strain – making hard work seem almost easy.

Affirmation:

Working hard on something I want is immensely satisfying.

Day 59

Making a success of the job at hand is the best step toward the kind you want.

- Bernard M. Baruch

This brilliant quote by Bernard M. Baruch serves as a great reminder that success is really a state of mind regardless of the actual activities we are doing at any given moment. We tend to think of success as it pertains to great achievements, but we can't expect to be successful at the big things if we aren't willing to give our best to what we are doing right now.

Whether we are walking the dog, paying bills, setting goals or writing a bestselling novel – making a success of everything we do guarantees that we will continue to evolve personally and professionally, reaching greater and greater levels of achievement for the rest of our lives.

Affirmation:

Giving my best effort makes me a success.

Day 60

Success is the ability to go from failure to failure without losing your enthusiasm.

- Winston Churchill

Keeping our enthusiasm high when facing challenges may seem impossible, especially when those challenges seem insurmountable. As Winston Churchill points out, however, simply choosing to stay enthusiastic and optimistic is what can ultimately make us successful.

Enthusiasm and other qualities of a positive attitude make obstacles appear to shrink in size and importance, buoying our confidence that we can overcome them. Even better, our confidence and optimism will usually help attract solutions we may not have considered from a negative state of mind. If we just refuse to lose hope or give up, success is inevitable.

Affirmation:

My success is guaranteed if I keep moving forward.

Day 61

No thought lives in your head rent free.

- Robert Allen

This brilliant quote by Robert Allen reminds us that there are consequences with everything – especially the thoughts we think on a daily basis. When it comes to negative or self-limiting thoughts, the consequences are clear: lack, struggle, frustration and stunted development on both personal and professional levels.

However, when we change the content of our thoughts to be more positive and empowering, not only do they "cost" less, they can actually "pay" us in the form of more money, joy, success, happiness, and a much deeper sense of satisfaction.

Affirmation:

I choose to allow only positive, empowering thoughts to reside in my mind.

Day 62

There is no security on this earth. There is only opportunity.

- Douglas MacArthur

Have you ever considered that the majority of things you do are based on a desire to feel secure? You may crave more income so you can feel secure about your financial status; you may dream of greater success because it usually includes career security; and so on.

The thing to remember, however, is that security is nothing more than a thought, belief or feeling that all is well. As Douglas MacArthur reminds us, security does not really exist – but opportunities do. No matter where we find ourselves right now, there exist endless opportunities for improvement – and that is truly the best kind of security.

Affirmation:

I am secure in my ability to handle anything.

Day 63

People are always blaming their circumstances for what they are. I don't believe in circumstances. The people who get on with this world are the people who get up and look for the circumstances they want, and, if they can't find them, make them.

- George Bernard Shaw

This sentiment by George Bernard Shaw may seem harsh at first glance, but it contains a powerful message for all of us. No matter where we have come from, no matter the difficult things that have happened to us, no matter the challenges and setbacks we have faced – we always have the power to start anew right now.

We simply need to look for the circumstances we want, and if we can't find them, make them. This may not be an easy task, but it is infinitely more empowering than continuing to believe in excuses and limitations. We set ourselves free by remembering that the only true limitations we face are in our own minds.

Affirmation:

I am strong enough to overcome any perceived limitation.

Day 64

Progress always involves risk. You can't steal second base and keep your foot on first.

- Frederick Wilcox

Taking a leap of faith is never easy, but that is why we call it a leap of "faith" – rather than a leap of certainty. Imagine how boring our lives would become if we only ever aimed for goals that had a predictable and certain outcome. With any endeavor, it is the thrill of risk that makes the rewards so sweet.

When it comes to your own goals and dreams, are you trying to move forward while also tightly gripping a safety line that prevents it? Are you afraid to let go of circumstances that no longer serve you? Give some thought to the pros and cons of taking a leap of faith and ask yourself if the rewards you would gain are worth the risk.

Affirmation:

Risks and rewards are nothing more than possibilities.

Day 65

You must not die with the dreadful feeling that your fears were greater than your dreams and that you never discovered what you really enjoy. You must know how to dare.

- Mark Fisher

There are few things that weigh as heavily on our minds as regrets. Opportunities not taken and goals that we never quite get up the courage to pursue do not fade away; they simply rest dormant in our hearts, urgently whispering that there is still time, it's not too late to try.

Ignoring these inner nudges only deepens a pervasive sense of dissatisfaction that will continue to spread throughout all areas of our lives. Eventually we realize that our fear of failure pales in comparison to the possibility of living the rest of our lives wondering what we could have achieved if we had simply tried.

Affirmation:

My dreams are much greater than my fears.

Day 66

A lack of money is never, ever, ever a problem.

- T. Harv Eker

Have you ever believed that a lack of money was a barrier when it came to pursuing your dreams and goals? It is true that many endeavors require money for certain phases, but a lack of money does not necessarily have to prevent you from moving forward in other ways before you reach that point.

Holding back because you do not yet have everything you need to reach your objectives is never helpful, and only strengthens the illusion of impossibility. Instead, make a long list of every aspect of your goals that do not require money to complete them, and then get moving on those aspects. As you do this, you inspire the universe to begin sending the other resources you will need, including money!

Affirmation:

Everything I need will come to me at the perfect time.

Day 67

Most people's lives are a direct reflection of their peer groups.

- Anthony Robbins

Have you ever considered that the people you spend most of your time with may be influencing your circumstances? As sociable creatures, we tend to gravitate toward people we feel most comfortable with – in other words, people that are much like ourselves. The problem is that by doing this we are cementing this "status" in our consciousness.

Improving yourself does not mean you have to turn away from the people you know and love – just that maybe you could spend a little more time focusing on and mingling with people who are as motivated and successful as you would like to be. If you don't know any of these people personally, read some inspiring biographies or watch documentaries about them. Exposing your consciousness to dynamic, successful people will positively influence your own self-image.

Affirmation:

I see my own success mirrored in other successful people.

Day 68

When the will comes in conflict with the imagination, the imagination invariably carries the day.

- Emile Coue

This intriguing quote by Emile Coue reminds us that willful desires can often cause trouble for us because they are products of the ego, while imagination is ruled by our intuition. When we find ourselves torn between these two opposing forces, it can be difficult to know the right course of action.

More often than not, following our intuition and allowing our imagination to lead the way is the wiser choice, simply because our will is usually rigid and inflexible, which can create immense frustration if outer events don't cooperate with our expectations. If we instead visualize the outcome we want and let go of how it all comes about, our imagination will easily inspire us to take the right actions to achieve it.

Affirmation:

I trust my intuition to pave the way to my desired outcome.

Day 69

The road to success is always under construction.

- Lily Tomlin

Lily Tomlin's humorous view of the "road to success" is quite accurate because no matter how precisely we plan our route, conditions change continuously and rarely do things turn out exactly the way we expect. However, problems arise when we base our perception of success on unrealistic expectations that the entire journey will be smooth and predictable.

Just like taking a road trip, we inevitably find that slight adjustments must be made all along the way – detouring from our initial plans and finding alternate routes when necessary. Getting angry about the delays and detours is pointless; as long as we arrive at the destination we intended when we began, that's all that matters in the end.

Affirmation:

I am taking the scenic route to success.

Day 70

The trouble with being poor is that it takes up all your time.

- Willem De Kooning

This illuminating quote powerfully reminds us that financial struggle has a way of penetrating nearly all areas of our lives in very destructive ways. When our minds are filled with thoughts of worry we have little energy or time to devote to anything else, even when other thoughts and activities would definitely serve us better.

One effective way to overcome persistent worrisome thoughts is to schedule periods of time where we do not allow our thoughts to run rampant with negative possibilities. During these periods we can instead focus on creative activities, daydream about things that inspire us, or even escape into a good book. Just by giving ourselves a break from worry, we often create a space for solutions to take root and grow.

Affirmation:

I choose to feel peaceful and inspired as often as I can.

Day 71

Opportunities repeat themselves because people repeat the same mistakes.

- Robert Kiyosaki

We often get frustrated when we keep repeating the same destructive patterns and getting the same dissatisfying results, but Robert Kiyosaki's insightful words serve as a great reminder that opportunities exist in every difficult circumstance. Rather than trying to escape negative situations, we would do better to ponder how we might turn them into something beneficial.

By focusing on the possibilities rather than the frustration, our creative juices start flowing and inspired ideas come rushing forth. Taking action on these inspired ideas will trigger still more opportunities, and before we know it our difficult circumstances will have been transformed into truly life-changing experiences.

Affirmation:

I am open to all possibilities for positive change.

Day 72

Ready, Fire, Aim! If you think too much about it, you may never start.

- Fred DeLuca and John P. Hayes

Over-analyzing goals and plans is a common destructive habit that many of us share. We plan, we prepare, plan some more…and never quite get around to taking action. Most often when this happens it's because we are trying to avoid the possibility of failure. It feels safer to wait until we have every step of the plan tweaked and adjusted "just right" before we move forward.

Unfortunately the longer we wait to get moving, the harder it gets to take any action at all. One of the most empowering habits we can adopt is a consistent willingness to move forward even if we don't yet have the entire plan figured out. Adjusting a plan that is already in motion is much easier than trying to create a "perfect" plan on paper.

Affirmation:

Knowing my next step is enough to keep making progress.

Day 73

In the business world, everyone is paid in two coins: cash and experience. Take the experience first; the cash will come later.

- Harold S. Geneen

This great quote by Harold S. Geneen can be applied to all areas of our lives, not just business. We have become so accustomed to seeing money as a success symbol that we forget there are other expressions of success – some of which are even more valuable than cash.

Experience may seem less important than money at first glance, but along with experience comes knowledge and self-mastery – which greatly enhances our earning potential in any field. Being patient enough to learn and gain experience so we can enjoy the fruits of our labor later is one of the best investments we can make into our future.

Affirmation:

The more I know, my wealth potential grows.

Day 74

No one can arrive from being talented alone. God gives talent; work transforms talent into genius.

- Anna Pavlova

It is easy to feel envious of talented, successful people until we realize that just having talent is not enough to create success by itself. We all have unique talents, but they do no good unless we hone them and share them with the world. Imagine a brilliant painter who was afraid to paint, or hid his art where no one could see it. Would he become successful? Probably not.

As Anna Pavlova reveals, work is what transforms mere talent into genius. Using our talents day by day and putting our creations out to the world begins to draw success toward us. Whether that success comes gradually or in one fell swoop does not matter; it matters only that we are willing to take a chance and create the right conditions for success.

Affirmation:

I confidently express my talents daily.

Day 75

I don't wait for moods. You accomplish nothing if you do that. Your mind must know it has to get down to work.

- Pearl S. Buck

One of the most common reasons we do not achieve goals is because our motivation naturally wanes over time. When we first set goals we are usually excited and confident that we can achieve them, and this inner fire keeps us moving forward for awhile. As our passion cools, however, we start making excuses and procrastinating, and eventually lose interest altogether.

The obvious solution is to develop a strong sense of self-discipline to stay accountable. Rather than waiting for the right mood to take hold of us, we can choose to strengthen our minds and do what needs to be done whether we feel like it or not. Interestingly, as we begin to make progress in this manner, we often find that our passion is re-ignited again and it gets easier to keep going.

Affirmation:

I am disciplined and focused, always.

Day 76

The key to success is to raise your own energy; when you do, people will naturally be attracted to you. And when they show up, bill em!

- Stuart Wilde

This humorous quote by Stuart Wilde contains a great nugget of truth: people respond to the energy we infuse into everything we do. Have you ever read a book or viewed a piece of artwork that seemed "flat" somehow; it just didn't seem to have that spark of inspiration that drew you forward and stirred your emotions? This usually happens when the creator of the work didn't put a lot of energy and passion into it.

Pouring the essence of passion and joy into your work is what will make it shine! It's the hidden ingredient that will draw people to you like moths to a flame, and yes – it is the same energy that will attract wealth and success beyond your wildest dreams. Whatever you do, do it with high energy. Pour as much love, joy, and passion into your work as you can and watch the magic happen.

Affirmation.

The more passionate I am, the more successful I am.

Day 77

If you want to get rich, you have to learn to earn.

- David Bach

This interesting line by David Bach could be interpreted in different ways, but one of the most powerful insights we can take from it is the importance of being willing to receive. It's funny that so many of us spend years dreaming of wealth and success – but feel guilty about charging money for our services or products, or receiving abundance in any form.

"Learning to earn" in this context would mean developing a strong belief that we deserve to be compensated for the work we do, and we deserve to be as wealthy and successful as we desire to be. Without a strong belief in our own deservingness, we are constantly broadcasting a split signal to the universe: "I want to be successful, but I don't deserve it." The universe doesn't judge; it simply gives us what we believe we deserve.

Affirmation:

I deserve great abundance and eagerly embrace it at every opportunity.

Day 78

There are two fools in this world. One is the millionaire who thinks that by hoarding money he can somehow accumulate real power, and the other is the penniless reformer who thinks that if only he can take the money from one class and give it to another, all the world's ills will be cured.

– Henry Ford

Henry Ford's wise words remind us that true power does not come from having money – and not having a lot of money does not make us powerless. It is easy to forget this crucial insight when we feel like our finances are lacking and wealthy people seem to have a much easier lifestyle. Eventually we learn that chasing money only keeps us feeling powerless and out of control.

Even worse, the more we chase after money the more it seems to elude us. When we take a step back from panic and frustration, we see that embracing our inner power and focusing on abundance will begin drawing money back toward us again. Before we know it, the universe begins dropping strong hints about the many ways we can keep our flow of abundance growing stronger and more consistent.

Affirmation:

Insight and focus are my real powers.

Day 79

We don't like their sound, and guitar music is on the way out.

– Decca Recording Co. rejecting the Beatles, 1962

Have you ever had what you thought was a great idea – but then rejected it because it seemed too outlandish, difficult, or ahead of its time? When you glimpse a quote like the one above through the clarity of hindsight, you realize how limiting pessimism and disbelief can be. Do you think the person(s) responsible for rejecting the Beatles regretted their hasty decision later?

Take a few minutes to consider some of your rejected ideas and goals from the past, and ask yourself if you may have been too hasty in dismissing them. If you dismissed them because you couldn't see any way to make them happen at the time, or you felt you didn't have access to the right resources, revisit the possibilities now and see if your outlook has changed. One of those ideas just might be the ticket to success you've been waiting for.

Affirmation:

I trust my hunches.

Day 80

If you can count your money, you don't have a billion dollars.

– J. Paul Getty

Do you know how many pairs of shoes are sitting in your closet right now? How about the number of forks and spoons you have in your kitchen drawers? Most of us don't have any idea how many pieces of other objects we have available at any given time, but we absolutely count every penny and keep a mental tally running when we spend or receive money.

This is part of being financially responsible, of course – but some of us watch our bank accounts from a position of fear and dread, which only slows down the flow of abundance through our lives. Like that old saying, "a watched pot never boils," our abundance will expand if we busy ourselves with other activities instead of hovering and worrying about how much we have.

Affirmation:

I am confident that I always have more than enough.

Day 81

I've never known any human being, high or humble, who ever regretted, when nearing life's end, having done kindly deeds. But I have known more than one millionaire who became haunted by the realization that they had led selfish lives.

– Barry C. Forbes

Barry Forbes reminds us of the importance of generosity with this quote, but the concept can be applied in a much bigger way than simply donating to charities and helping the less fortunate. The most important point of this quote is tagged on at the very end with the reference to "selfish lives". Selfishness is not reserved for the rich – and it has nothing to do with how much money we keep or donate.

Instead, let us see these words as an indication of attitude. A person with a selfish attitude would most likely be continuously focused on what they stand to gain from every situation, whereas an unselfish person would be focused on what they can offer or share in every situation. Believe it or not, the unselfish focus can make you wealthy much faster and easier than the selfish attitude could.

Affirmation:

I choose to focus on what I can offer others.

Day 82

Success is simply a matter of luck. Ask any failure.

– Earl Wilson

This tongue-in-cheek quote by Earl Wilson offers an important insight into the perception that our ability to achieve success or failure is out of our hands. Whether we chalk it up to "luck" or simply being in the right place at the right time, we often hold a subconscious belief that we aren't really in control of our own destiny.

We need to keep reminding ourselves that the thing that determines success or failure is the willingness to keep working at it until we get where we want to be. If we quit, we can easily find dozens of excuses for why we failed (bad luck being one of them) – but deep inside we'll know that luck had nothing to do with it.

Affirmation:

My good luck charm is called "persistence."

Day 83

Every really new idea looks crazy at first.

– Alfred North Whitehead

Limited thinking is one of the ways we subconsciously hold ourselves back from truly great achievements in life. Stepping out of our comfort zones can be frightening, so we tend to set goals that will move us just slightly beyond where we are now. While this approach can make our goals appear more manageable, it is also restrictive and keeps us in a perpetual state of dissatisfaction.

What if, for just one day, we decided to throw caution to the wind and dare to dream as big as we possibly could? What if we looked at our present goals and aspirations – and then expanded our vision of them so they were one thousand times bigger? Gathering the courage to see our dreams in this way virtually guarantees that we will accomplish ten times more than we would have by limiting ourselves.

Affirmation:

Just for today I choose to believe that I can achieve my "crazy ideas".

Day 84

A penny saved is a penny earned.

– Benjamin Franklin

When most of us think of wealth, we imagine greater amounts of money flowing into our lives, which will then create greater financial freedom. However, sometimes we forget another crucial aspect of financial wellness: managing the money we already have in responsible ways. Poor money management can be just as destructive and frustrating as inadequate cash flow.

Today take some time to consider whether you may have unnecessary financial "drains" that are reducing your bottom line. Do you still pay for old memberships that you no longer use? Do you wonder where your money goes every month because you don't track your spending? Plugging these "holes" can make you feel richer because you end up keeping more of the money you already have.

Affirmation:

Saving money attracts more money.

Day 85

You have to make contacts to get contacts.

– Cavett Robert

One of the more intimidating aspects of improving our lives is the necessity of putting ourselves "out there" and attracting more clients, customers, or opportunities for growth. This insightful quote by Cavett Robert reminds us that networking is a vital part of growth. Whether we are trying to grow our business or simply seeking support and motivation for our personal goals, we usually make much faster progress if we reach out and join forces with others.

The secret to forming beneficial partnerships is twofold: first being clear about what we hope to gain from the partnership, and secondly, believing that we have something of equal value to offer our partner(s). When these two conditions are met, we enter into a mutually beneficial flow of give and take - and dynamic, consistent growth is inevitable.

Affirmation:

I confidently align myself with likeminded people.

Day 86

Don't go around saying the world owes you a living; the world owes you nothing; it was here first.

– Mark Twain

As Mark Twain brilliantly points out, there is a fine line between deservingness and an inflated sense of entitlement. Entitlement means that we want everything for nothing – we want the world (or great wealth) handed to us on a silver platter without offering anything of value to the world in return. (Often because we don't believe we have anything of value to offer.)

True deservingness, on the other hand, is a much more flexible state of mind where we believe we deserve to be wealthy and content, but we are also eager to help others achieve the same success. We are willing to work hard, be patient, give our best effort to everything we do, knowing all the while that we will be richly rewarded for it – and with such a positive attitude, we always are.

Affirmation:

Today I expand my awareness of my own deservingness.

Day 87

The first rule is not to lose. The second rule is not to forget the first rule.

– Warren Buffet

We often see the events of our lives in black and white terms – either we win or we lose. Warren Buffet's words appear to be in line with that concept, until we consider that "losing" can have many different meanings. Losing is often perceived to be the exact opposite of winning; in other words, failing to achieve a favorable outcome in a given situation.

However, who gets to decide what "a favorable outcome" is? One of the best habits we can adopt is to consciously take something positive away from every experience. Even the most difficult and trying circumstances offer a great lesson, a new opportunity, or a chance to reflect and refine our goals. If we learn to view all of our experiences in this way, we quickly realize that we "win" no matter what else is happening around us.

Affirmation:

I adopt a winning attitude in everything I do.

Day 88

Wealth is not his that has it, but his that enjoys it.

– Benjamin Franklin

Wealth can be defined in many ways, both monetary and otherwise, but most of us tend to equate wealth with having millions of dollars in the bank. Believing in this ideal makes us feel safe and secure, like everything else in our lives would fall magically into place if we just had enough money to buffer us from potential misfortune.

The truth is, no matter how much money we are able to accumulate, we will never feel truly wealthy until we learn to live rich lives. Living a rich life means taking pleasure from every moment, always trusting that we have more than enough, striving for greater and greater accomplishments, and continuing to grow and develop ourselves on all levels. Interestingly, we usually discover that we can do this even without having millions of dollars in the bank.

Affirmation:

I choose to enjoy the many expressions of wealth in my life right now.

Day 89

Rich people keep their commitment.

– T. Harv Eker

Everyone has commitments regardless of how much money we have, but this quote can speak powerfully to another aspect of commitment: committing to our vision. Most of us are committed to achieving our goals and improving our finances when we first conceive the desire, but external events can often shake our determination.

Noticing that we aren't making as much progress as we hoped, or running into obstacle after obstacle can tempt us to give up because the situation seems so hopeless. However, if we learn to see the completion of our vision as an ironclad obligation, we find it easier to push through the rough spots and persevere. One of the definitions of "commit" is "to carry into action". By that definition, continuing to move forward and keep trying is keeping our commitment.

Affirmation:

Day 90

If you think education is expensive try ignorance.

– Benjamin Franklin

Have you ever held back on investing in your own development because of the expense involved? Perhaps you stumbled upon a great business course you wanted to take but financial pressures convinced you it should wait, or you wanted to go back to school and earn your degree but cringed at the time investment required.

What we often fail to see in situations like these is that we stand to gain so much more than we expend by investing in ourselves. As Benjamin Franklin cleverly suggests, ignorance can act as a cancer that spreads throughout every aspect of our lives, limiting our progress in endless ways. It may not always be easy to obtain the resources we need to keep bettering ourselves, but the time, energy and money we invest will continue to pay off for the rest of our lives.

Affirmation:

I am a worthwhile investment.

Day 91

All progress has resulted from people who take unpopular positions.

– Adlai Stevenson

So many of us have been taught to keep a low profile in the world; don't make waves, don't cause a scene, don't upset the status quo . . . But when we look at some of the most influential and successful people in the world, we see that their achievements came about when they stepped off the beaten path and forged their own way.

How many of your own actions are based on the fear that others won't like what you're doing? Living your life according to these ideals can only lead to frustration and stunted growth. Today take some time to think about what YOU want. What do you stand for? What's important to you? Then use these insights to step off the beaten path and forge a brand new beginning with courage and determination – regardless of how unpopular your position may seem.

Affirmation:

I stand strong in my convictions.

Day 92

Someday this will be true of all of us: our network will equal our net worth.

– Tim Sanders

When it comes to money and business, the connections we make with others are often the most valuable assets we have. The larger and more diverse our network of clients, customers and colleagues, the more opportunities we have to grow and prosper. While success is certainly a product of positive attitude, hard work and determination, we can't do it all on our own.

Each one of us needs a network that lends support, encouragement, insight and resources that we can use to keep growing. Creating this network is as simple as reaching out to share our own support, encouragement, insight and resources with others – and as we do this consistently we find that the very same thing is instantly reflected back to us from others.

Affirmation:

As I reach out, others reach back to me.

Day 93

Never take counsel of your fears.

– General Stonewall Jackson

This famous quote seems simple at first glance, but there is a deeper meaning if we look a little closer. Most of us know that fear can be destructive in holding us back from pursuing our goals and dreams, but General Jackson's message reveals an even bigger hindrance in the words, "take counsel". How often do you make decisions based on fear, doubt or uncertainty? How much of your life is built upon attempts to avoid fearful possibilities?

"Taking counsel of your fears" means allowing fear to inspire your actions – or inaction. Imagine how much more empowering it would be to take counsel of your inspiration, courage, imagination and determination. Imagine basing your actions on the wonderful possibilities, rather than the frightening ones. It's easy to see the power and potential that would result.

Affirmation:

Inspiration and courage are my counselors.

Day 94

Attempt the impossible only to improve your work.

– Bette Davis

We usually set goals with the objective of achieving a specific outcome, but Bette Davis offers another powerful motivator: improving the quality and magnitude of our work. Seeing our goals in this light can not only be empowering but also fantastically liberating. Rather than setting a goal and hoping and praying that we'll get the results we want, we can simply focus on strengthening our skills and talents with every step we take.

As we do this, we ease the pressure we feel to succeed at all costs and instead allow success to flow naturally as we grow and develop our skills. Attempting the impossible is one sure way to stretch beyond our comfort zones and see our true capabilities – and every time we do this we discover that we are capable of much more than we suspected.

Affirmation:

I love to challenge myself by attempting the impossible.

Day 95

Today's preparation determines tomorrow's achievement.

– Unknown

We often think of preparation as a way to avoid potential problems, like creating an "emergency fund" for unexpected financial shortages, or exploring other career options when rumors of potential downsizing begin circulating. This is certainly a responsible practice, but there is also another way to use preparation to our advantage – by preparing for success.

Many of us still view success as a byproduct of luck or random chance, despite knowing the true power of thoughts, beliefs, and focused action. Rather than taking tentative action and "hoping" we succeed, we could prepare for success by firmly believing that we will succeed, being confident and deliberate in our movements, networking with highly successful people, and refusing to entertain the possibility of failure at all.

Affirmation:

As I prepare for success, I become a magnet for it.

Day 96

The will to win is worthless if you do not have the will to prepare.

– Thand Yost

When you think about having great wealth and prosperity, you probably imagine that you would enjoy a much more relaxed lifestyle than you do now. However, ask yourself: would you truly be comfortable managing large sums of money? Having plenty of money does not automatically generate feelings of peace and well-being – in fact it can lead to chronic stress and frustration if you don't first prepare your mind for greater abundance.

One of the best ways to do this is to mentally imagine having plenty of money and feeling relaxed and comfortable about it. How would the people in your life react if you were wealthy? How would you handle requests for money from friends and loved ones? How would you keep your money organized? Thinking about these things in advance can make your transition into abundance much smoother and less frightening.

Affirmation:

Every day I get more comfortable with the idea of being wealthy.

Day 97

You can't make someone else's choices. You shouldn't let someone else make yours.

– Colin Powell

Most of us understand the futility of allowing others to run our lives, but few of us realize how much influence our family, friends, and colleagues have over our financial success. Much of this influence is subtle, yet powerful – like worrying how our friends would react if we suddenly became very successful, or being hesitant about buying a new car because the neighbors might think we are showing off.

The only effective way to deal with these types of fears is to acknowledge that we can't control the feelings or behavior of other people. If our wealth and success cause people we thought were friends to turn away from us or talk badly about us, we can't do much about it. What we can do is align ourselves with likeminded people who are determined to create better lives and will support and encourage us as we strive to do the same.

Affirmation:

I choose to surround myself with supportive people.

Day 98

The purpose of life is to believe, to hope, and to strive.

– Indira Gandhi

This beautiful quote by Indira Gandhi offers an important reminder about the power of a hopeful attitude. Discouragement has killed many a dream throughout the ages, but it usually happens when people stop hoping and believing that their dreams can be realized. Unfortunately, once hope is gone so is any possibility of success.

However, if we were to make hope and belief the very purpose of our lives rather than attaching them to a specific outcome, our dreams would never die. Perhaps they would change form and direction over time, but we would always have a reason to keep believing, hoping, and striving – no matter the obstacles and setbacks we encountered.

Affirmation:

My hope and belief grow stronger every day.

Day 99

We are indeed much more than what we eat, but what we eat can nevertheless help us to be much more than what we are.

- Adelle Davis

Adelle Davis may be referring to nutrition and physical wellness with these words, but the same concept could easily be applied to our wealth mindset too. Just as the quality of food we eat has an effect on our physical bodies, the quality of our thoughts determines our mindset, which also has an effect on our material abundance.

What has your "mental diet" looked like for most of your life? Have you been feeding your mind heaping portions of "junk food" in the form of pessimism, negativity, and limiting beliefs? Have you become heavily invested in the limitations that others have placed on you? If so, you should find that gradually improving the quality of your mental diet will help you to become much more than you currently are - and everything around you must shift to match who you are.

Affirmation:

I feed my mind with thoughts of love, success, abundance and ease.

Day 100

I need no warrant for being, and no word of sanction upon my being. I am the warrant and the sanction.

- Ayn Rand

Many people approach the manifestation process backwards, by trying to obtain or achieve something on the outside, which they believe will make them feel better on the inside. However, these powerful words by Ayn Rand remind us that we are the very things we seek. We do not need to seek wealth, or success, or happiness; they are already here. We simply need to claim them and become the person who has them.

How do we do this? By mentally shifting our awareness to encompass the existence of the things we want to experience. In other words, if we want to have more abundance, we need to BE wealthy now. Feel as if we are already wealthy. Act as if we are wealthy. Speak as if we are wealthy. Anything else will contradict our belief that we already have it and continue to push wealth away from us.

Affirmation:

I choose to BE happy, healthy and wealthy now.

Day 101

Every time we say, "Let there be!" in any form, something happens.

- Stella Terrill Mann

There's no doubt about it; our expectations hold great power. Stella Terrill Mann reminds us that simply setting forth a strong intention can often be enough to set energy in motion and create dramatic changes in our lives. Unfortunately, this same power of expectation can often work against us if we fail to use it deliberately.

For example, how many times have you prepared for the worst even though you were hoping for a positive result? How often have you abandoned a goal or dream because there seemed to be no way to make it happen? Every time you do this, you are saying, "Let there be," and intending the very outcome you do not want. Instead, begin saying frequently, "Let there be abundance! Let there be success! Let there be joy!" and allow the universe to help you make it happen.

Affirmation:

I expect only the outcomes I want to experience.

Day 102

Associate with well-mannered persons and your manners will improve. Run around with decent folk and your own decent instincts will be strengthened.

- Stanley Walker

There is a popular theory that we are the sum total of the people we spend the most time with, and Stanley Walker's insight seems to underscore that point. The problem with this theory is that most of us do not have access to the kind of people we want to emulate. We can't simply pick up the phone to invite Bill Gates or Donald Trump to dinner. What we can do, however, is use the power of imagination to create these beneficial associations.

We can imagine playing golf with Tiger Woods, working on an exciting charitable project with Oprah Winfrey, or doing a fun cooking show with Rachel Ray. We aren't limited to real people either - we can just as easily create imaginary successful people and envision ourselves working and playing with them each day. The more we do this, the more our minds will be exposed to images of success, wealth and progress, and begin replaying them in our physical reality.

Affirmation:

I am a magnet for wealthy, successful people.

Day 103

Indolence is a delightful but distressing state; we must be doing something to be happy.

- Mahatma Gandhi

Do you ever take action for the sheer joy of doing something, or are the bulk of your actions taken simply because they will move you forward? Most of us have been trained to see action as a means to an end. If we want to be wealthy and successful, we must take the actions that will bring about the result. The problem with this approach is that we don't allow ourselves to feel happy until we have reached the goal.

As Mahatma Gandhi suggests above, what if we were to begin seeing action itself as a way to be happy? What if we began to take action simply because it makes us feel purposeful and productive? What if we let go of the belief that we can't be happy unless this or that happens? Not only would such an attitude virtually guarantee a positive outcome, it would make the entire journey much more enjoyable.

Affirmation:

I choose to enjoy every step of my journey.

Day 104

Love flies, runs, and rejoices; it is free and nothing can hold it back.

- Thomas a Kempis

It is said that love is one of the most powerful forces in the universe, and this is especially evident in our state of financial wellness. When it comes to money, most of us have created a powerful love/hate relationship. We want more money to come to us, but often don't appreciate the money we do have. We love the thought of having financial freedom, but we resent the people who appear to have it already.

One effective way to neutralize this love/hate energy in your own life is to start blessing and affirming every positive expression of abundance you can. Mentally bless wealthy people and feel happy for their good fortune. Give thanks for every penny you have, and love the possibility of more arriving soon. The more completely you can love every expression of abundance, the more frequently it will begin showing up in your life.

Affirmation:

I love seeing abundance everywhere I go.

Day 105

There are some things you learn best in calm, and some in storm.

- Willa Cather

Often it seems that just when you're starting to make progress, a crisis will arrive and create great upheaval in your life. This is especially true when you begin altering your existing beliefs about money and abundance. The circumstances of your life are built upon your existing beliefs, and changing that foundation can often trigger what appear to be negative events.

However, when you look a little closer at these supposed negative events, you may realize that they are paving the way for even better circumstances later. In order to make room for the better conditions you desire, you may need to first endure the falling away of limiting or unhealthy situations that no longer serve you. Choosing to see these experiences as opportunities to grow and become stronger can enrich your understanding and make the transition much easier.

Affirmation:

I embrace the changes that help me grow wiser and stronger.

Day 106

After all it is those who have a deep and real inner life who are best able to deal with the irritating details of outer life.

- Evelyn Underhill

Improving the quality of our thoughts and beliefs can help attract better experiences into our lives, but this does not mean that the outer aspects of our lives will magically transform into perfect order and we will live "happily ever after". Despite a positive attitude there will always be things we cannot control, like the actions of other people for example.

As Evelyn Underhill shares above, the true gift of a positive mindset is the ability to better handle life's "irritating details". Our reaction to those details is what often determines the final outcome. Reacting with anger and frustration only fuels the negative energy and keeps it going. Keeping our composure and staying positive, on the other hand, is often enough to inspire creative solutions and contribute to the formation of pleasant surprises later.

Affirmation:

I handle adversity with a calm and happy attitude.

Day 107

Never read a book through merely because you have begun it.

- John Witherspoon

John Witherspoon's wise words serve as a great reminder that it's never too late to change direction – no matter how far we have traveled upon our current path. Have you ever set a goal and begun working toward it, only to realize a short time later that you weren't enjoying the process and you were quickly losing the motivation to keep going?

Forcing yourself to push forward despite a lack of passion is like forcing yourself to finish reading a dry, boring book. Today, take a few minutes to examine your existing goals closely. Do you still feel as excited about them as you did at the start? If not, perhaps you can modify them or set completely new goals to get your creative juices flowing again. When you feel passionate about what you're doing, motivation comes naturally.

Affirmation:

I choose goals that fill me with joy and passion.

Day 108

A preoccupation with the future not only prevents us from seeing the present as it is but often prompts us to rearrange the past.

- Eric Hoffer

One of the biggest challenges in learning to use the Law of Attraction deliberately is having the presence of mind to focus on something other than what we are living right now. Rather than focusing on financial lack and struggle, we need to retrain our minds to see abundance, believe in abundance, and imagine having abundance. However, doing this can also tempt us to negate the positive aspects of our past and present experiences.

Our past and present experiences may not seem to be all that great at times but they have provided opportunities to learn and grow, and therefore hold great value. Rather than trying to deny our past and present, a better balance might be to focus on creating a better future while also choosing to feel happy and grateful for what we have now, and the past experiences (both good and bad) that have helped us to become who we are.

Affirmation:

My past, present, and future are all good in their own ways.

Day 109

The best years of your life are the ones in which you decide your problems are your own. You don't blame them on your mother, the ecology, or the President. You realize that you control your own destiny.

- Albert Ellis

As you look at your current life circumstances, do you feel tempted to blame their existence on other people, companies, or forces beyond your control? Like most people, you may want to resist believing that you are the only one who has created these conditions. However, there is an easy way to accept this possibility without blame or self-recrimination: By reminding yourself that the creation process is largely subconscious for the majority of us.

Now that you are learning more about the way your thoughts and feelings affect your physical reality, you are in a much better position to consciously create your life from this point on. But you cannot berate yourself for not knowing better in the past. Taking responsibility for your life is not about self-blame. Instead, see it as an opportunity to choose something better because you now have the knowledge and strength to do so.

Affirmation:

I acknowledge my ability to do better now.

Day 110

The law is not so much carved in stone as it is written in water, flowing in and out with the tide.

- Jeff Melvoin

When trying to attract greater abundance it is easy to get stuck in rigid thinking about the right and wrong ways to achieve our goal. We are told that we must visualize daily; we must give to receive; we must recite affirmations, and so on. All of these activities have merit, but they are really secondary to the main goal: improving the quality of our "frequency."

Improving the quality of the frequency we emit to the universe is as simple as thinking positively more often than we think negatively; feeling happy instead of angry; focusing on abundance more than we focus on scarcity. Even if we never recited a single affirmation or visualized a hefty bank balance, simply thinking, speaking and acting in more positive ways would be enough to attract a generous flow of abundance through our lives. We can choose to make wealth attraction an easy process just as easily as we can make it hard on ourselves.

Affirmation:

My happy mindset attracts abundance easily.

Day 111

True humor is fun - it does not put down, kid, or mock. It makes people feel wonderful, not separate, different, and cut off. True humor has beneath it the understanding that we are all in this together.

- Hugh Prather

Humor is one of the most powerful ways to attract more abundance into your life, but sadly most of us do not deliberately seek opportunities to laugh and feel good. Do you spend most of your days focused on work and other obligations? Does it sometimes feel like you're stuck in a rut of boredom or stress?

The key is to seek humor that you find funny. We are all different because we have such unique life perspectives. Think about the kind of movies, books, and activities that lift your spirits and make you laugh, and then set aside time each day to enjoy yourself. If you start making laughter a priority in your life, you should find that your mood improves, which improves the signal you send to the universe – which should also return abundance and many good things back to you.

Affirmation:

Laughter feeds my heart, mind and wallet.

Day 112

No one else can speak the words on your lips.
Drench yourself in words unspoken. Live your life
with arms wide open. Today is where your book
begins. The rest is still unwritten.

- Natasha Bedingfield

One of the most important things to do when trying
to attract better life circumstances is to get very
clear on what you want. This may seem simple,
but it can be difficult because so many of us are
heavily conditioned by our loved ones, society, and
even our own limiting beliefs. Often we won't allow
ourselves to acknowledge what we REALLY want
because we don't believe it's possible for us to
have it.

Take a moment to think about your existing goals
right now. Are those the outcomes you truly want?
If you had no limitations whatsoever, are those
situations and experiences what you would choose
– or have you been limiting yourself according to
your beliefs or other people's perceptions about
what is possible for you? As Natasha Bedingfield
proposes, you can write any chapter you like into
your "book" – but first you have to decide what
you'd like to see there.

Affirmation:

I expand my perception of what is possible for my
life.

Day 113

The strongest possible piece of advice I would give any young woman is: Don't screw around, and don't smoke.

- Edwina Currie

Edwina Currie's blunt words share a strong message about the importance of self-respect, which is also important when it comes to your ability to attract greater abundance into your life. Have you ever allowed someone to take advantage of you? Do you often acquiesce to the demands of others even though they conflict with your own preferences? Are you asking for abundance and then acting in ways that tell the universe you don't believe you deserve it?

Developing a strong sense of self-respect can trigger some surprising and welcome changes in your life – especially when it comes to expressions of abundance. When you refuse to accept mistreatment from others; refuse to settle for less than you deserve; and believe in your own value and worthiness, the universe will deliver experiences that mesh with your inner perception. This can include more money, meaningful relationships, better health, and much more.

Affirmation:

I allow myself to receive only goodness in every possible way.

Day 114

Perfectionism is simply putting a limit on your future. When you have an idea of perfect in your mind, you open the door to constantly comparing what you have now with what you want. That type of self criticism is significantly deterring.

- John Eliot, Ph.D.

Have you ever felt like you were walking on eggshells when trying to attract better life circumstances? Do you ever fear that you may be "doing it wrong," or that a few minutes of negative thinking can undo all of the progress you've made? It's important to remember that you cannot get this process wrong. The Law of Attraction does not see things as right or wrong.

Instead, try to see this process as a continual unfolding of your dominant focus. The more you practice, the easier it will be to stay in a state of joy and gratitude. The more you work at aligning your thoughts and emotions, the better your circumstances will get. And if you have a rough day now and then, don't worry that you've messed up the process. Simply get back to the basics and continue taking one step at a time. As the old saying goes, strive for progress, not perfection.

Affirmation:

I get clearer, stronger and better every day.

Day 115

We cannot fail to win unless we fail to try.

- Tom Clancy

Have you ever held yourself back from setting bigger goals because you were afraid you might fail to achieve them? After one or more painful failures early in our lives, most of us decided to squelch down our dreams and settle for "safer" endeavors so we never have to feel that way again. Unfortunately, such a habit only keeps us feeling dissatisfied. If you want to expand your perceived limitations in a fun and easy way, try the following exercise.

Grab a notebook and pen and find a quiet place to be alone. Clear your mind and then try to imagine the biggest, grandest goal for your life that you can. Make big enough that you have no idea how to make it happen, but still realistic enough so that you can see yourself living it. Write this goal down in detail, ask the universe to show you how to make it happen, and then stay alert to any insights or nudges you may get about actions that would move you toward achieving it. By expanding your realm of possibilities in this way, you minimize any fear of failure and make success much more likely.

Affirmation:

I allow myself to dream big and achieve the success I deserve.

Day 116

Look not mournfully into the past. It comes not back again. Wisely improve the present. It is thine. Go forth to meet the shadowy future, without fear.

- Henry Wadsworth Longfellow

When trying to attract better circumstances, it's important to keep in mind that it's easier to attract a brand-new condition than it is to fix or remake something that already exists. The circumstances of your life are here because of your past thoughts and beliefs, and you cannot change the things you thought and believed in the past.

What you can do, however, is begin thinking and believing differently today. As you think and believe in a new way, you will begin forming new circumstances that better suit your current desires. Even better, remember that your current circumstances were probably created by default. Now that you know how to choose something better, you will have much more control over what appears in your life in the future.

Affirmation:

I eagerly look forward to a better, richer future.

Day 117

Talent is nothing but a prolonged period of attention and shortened period of mental assimilation.

- Konstantin Stanislavsky

It's easy to forget that people who appear to be talented have usually devoted an extraordinary amount of time and energy into developing that talent. As Konstantin Stanislavsky points out, focusing your attention on something for an extended period of time helps you to understand and assimilate the knowledge more easily. Over time, that task or activity becomes like second nature and seems almost easy to do, simply because you've done it so many times before.

The very same process is used to master your ability to create your life circumstances consciously. Once you understand that your thoughts, emotional state and beliefs all work together to attract corresponding events and experiences, you know exactly what to do to create the kind of life you want. First, however, there must be a practice period that allows you to develop your talent and keep working at it, until eventually it will get easier and easier.

Affirmation:

Every moment is an opportunity to hone my talent as a deliberate creator.

Day 118

Train yourself to let go of the things you fear to lose.

- George Lucas

Detachment is a crucial part of the attraction process that is seldom discussed, and unfortunately it is one of the things that many of us struggle with daily. The ego mind does not like to let go because it fears being deprived of the things it thinks it needs to feel happy. Each of us has an ego mind, and it is this part of us that often throws a wrench into the attraction process and causes unnecessary delays.

As George Lucas suggests above, training yourself to let go is important - and this is especially true when it comes to the things you are trying to attract into your life. The reason for this is simple: The more tightly you cling to something, the stronger signals of "need" and "lack" you are communicating to the universe, which can only create more instances of need and lack. On the other hand, when you let go and trust, you communicate a sense of all being well, which the universe will also replicate in your life.

Affirmation:

I let go and trust that everything I need will arrive with perfect timing.

Day 119

Although the world is full of suffering, it is full also of the overcoming of it.

- Helen Keller

More often than not, the things that cause us the most pain are not the situations and experiences of our lives, but our reactions to them. In our attempt to fight against, struggle with, and overcome our problems, we end up exacerbating them! Rather than fighting against our problems, we can use the Law of Attraction to rise above them and shift smoothly and easily into better circumstances.

Are you currently struggling with a situation or condition that is causing you pain and suffering? Decide right now that you are going to release it and rise above it mentally and emotionally. Rather than trying to fix the situation or force things to go the way you want, simply turn your thoughts to a better condition and imagine that it already exists. Imagine that you can attune to it simply by dropping the struggle and adjusting your focus. Then watch in awe as seemingly insurmountable obstacles are dissolved and the path before you becomes clear again.

Affirmation:

Today I rise above struggle and attune to peace.

Day 120

*The minute you settle for less than you deserve,
you get even less than you settled for.*

- Maureen Dowd

Maureen Dowd's insightful words remind us of the necessity of truly believing that we deserve the things we are asking for. Low self-worth is a chronic problem for many people – and the most challenging thing about it is that we may not even realize we have it! The good news is that there is an easy way to tell if low self-worth may be hindering your ability to attract what you want. Right now, think about something you want and have been trying to attract.

Then grab a sheet of paper and write down, "I deserve to have (fill in your desire here)." Read that statement to yourself a few times, and notice how you feel. If you really do believe you deserve it, you will feel calm and confident about it. If you are holding any resistance to that belief you will feel a twinge of guilt, doubt, uncertainty, or fear pop up. This is a clear sign that you need to work on strengthening your belief that you deserve the things you want.

Affirmation:

I choose to believe that I am worthy.

Day 121

You can't turn back the clock. But you can wind it up again.

- Bonnie Prudden

Do you ever struggle to find the time to meditate, journal, visualize or otherwise work on attracting the things you want? It seems that as we keep getting busier it gets more and more challenging to set aside time for ourselves. You may be pleased to know that you don't need to spend hours in meditation to create a better life for yourself.

Merely setting aside 10 or 15 minutes daily to clear your mind, visualize something wonderful, or keep a gratitude journal can go a long way in improving your state of mind. You can also perform mini-visualizations as you go about your daily activities. Simply muse and ponder a pleasant scenario for a few minutes, like having plenty of money in the bank, paying your bills with ease, and so on. You are still emitting positive vibrations out to the universe and attracting corresponding experiences!

Affirmation:

I make great progress by taking small, consistent steps toward my goal.

Day 122

I can accept failure, but I can't accept not trying.

- Michael Jordan

As you work on attracting greater abundance into your life, it's important to keep in mind that your efforts should focus on the quality of energy and intention you put forth, not just the number of activities you can squeeze into your day. Many people are under the impression that by using techniques like affirmations, visualization, and vision boards they are doing everything needed to attract better conditions in their lives, but that is not necessarily true.

If they use those tools halfheartedly or scatter their energy too much, their results will show it. Remember that those tools are designed to help you create the right intensity of focus, which is what really triggers positive changes in your life. You can make more progress from 10 minutes of highly focused visualization than from weeks of scattered, halfhearted efforts. As Michael Jordan suggests above, "trying" is important – but your clarity of intent is even more important.

Affirmation:

I give every activity my full effort and attention.

Day 123

The power of imagination makes us infinite.

- John Muir

John Muir's insightful statement reveals the key to creating your life on purpose: imagination. Imagination is truly one of the most powerful tools in your manifestation toolbox. Through the power of your imagination, you can instantly become as wealthy as you desire. You can become a successful author, speaker, or activist. You can meet the love of your life, build your dream home, drive any car you like – and much more. As John Muir says, the power of your imagination truly makes you infinite – which means limitless, boundless, endless.

Of course, forming these visions into tangible creations in physical reality takes a healthy dose of belief, trust and patience. Most likely your new and improved reality will not magically manifest overnight, and the finished result may not be exactly as you envisioned it. But if you are willing to work in partnership with the universe, you will realize that the visions you conceived in your imagination were only tiny seeds holding the bigger potential for you and your life.

Affirmation:

My inner vision gives birth to a greater reality.

Day 124

First say to yourself what you would be; and then do what you have to do.

- Epictetus

Many of us approach the attraction process backwards by believing that having a lot of money will make us feel wealthy; having a passionate relationship will make us feel loved; and having a great career will make us feel successful. Epictetus reminds us that it actually works the other way around. By first BEING the wealthy, lovable, successful person we want to be, we cannot help but think and act in ways that will draw those exact circumstances to us.

Consider the behavioral difference between a person with a wealth mindset and a person with a poverty mindset. A person who is focused on lack and hardship would automatically think and act in ways that continue to reinforce conditions of scarcity and struggle. On the other hand, a person focused on wealth and abundance would always act in ways that perpetuate the reality of a prosperous, joyful existence. You choose either of these realities through the power of your focus – your ability to choose who you are "being" in every moment.

Affirmation:

I choose to be wealthy, successful and happy now.

Day 125

Along with success comes a reputation for wisdom.

- Euripides

Successful people are often thought to be wise because they have mastered the process of right thought and right action, which creates a favorable result. However, there is another aspect of success that can also convey a reputation for wisdom, and that is demeanor. Have you ever noticed that successful people carry themselves differently than most unsuccessful or struggling people do? Struggling people appear to be weighed down, stressed and depressed; while successful people exude confidence, capability, and a powerful sense of self-belief.

The body language of successful people seems to scream, "I am strong, I am powerful, I can do anything, I deserve the best that life has to offer – and I will not settle for less!" Needless to say, this very attitude is communicated to the universe as an intention, and the universe simply delivers events and experiences that correspond with it. From this moment on, paying close attention to your demeanor will help you to be sure that your unspoken intention to the universe is one that you want to be reflected into your physical surroundings.

Affirmation:

I convey wisdom, success and empowerment as my unspoken intention.

Day 126

They can because they think they can.

- Virgil

Believing in yourself is vitally important when it comes to achieving goals, simply because you won't give your full effort if you think there is a chance you might fail. However, there is a big difference between "thinking" and "knowing" that you can do something. For example, you probably think that you could climb a mountain if you trained and prepared accordingly. But in the moment you attempt to do it, you would probably begin to have serious doubts about your ability. That's because you don't "know" that you can do it if you've never done it before.

The same goes for anything you attempt to do, like attracting great wealth into your life. Logically you may think you can do it – but do you really believe it, deep down inside? Or do you have twinges of doubt about your ability? Overcoming feelings of doubt is as simple as building up your confidence and moving forward anyway. With every step, the doubt begins to fade and your belief in yourself grows stronger – and your results will also grow in proportion to that belief.

Affirmation:

I choose to act as if I can accomplish anything I desire.

Day 127

Nothing can stop the man with the right mental attitude from achieving his goal; nothing on earth can help the man with the wrong mental attitude.

- Thomas Jefferson

Most of us are taught that taking focused action is what will move us toward our goals, but using the Law of Attraction requires a slightly different approach. Action is certainly an important part of manifesting the things we want – but most of us learn quickly that taking action without first getting our thoughts and beliefs in alignment is an exercise in futility. In fact, you have probably experienced the frustration that comes from taking massive action day after day and still getting absolutely nowhere.

As Thomas Jefferson proposes, attitude is everything – and nowhere is this truer than in context with the Law of Attraction. Without positive intention and belief, your action steps will likely be fruitless. But with a positive mental attitude, opportunities and successful outcomes seem to flow into your life easily and frequently. The right people, circumstances and resources simply appear before you with perfect timing. And the actions you do take from such a positive mental state cannot help but be more fruitful than they would have been if taken from a negative state of mind.

Affirmation:

The right mindset makes action seem effortless.

Day 128

Success is the sum of small efforts, repeated day in and day out.

- Robert Collier

One of the more challenging aspects of learning to create better circumstances with the Law of Attraction is remembering to work at it consistently, day after day. Just as success takes time to build, so does great abundance. When we approach the attraction process halfheartedly we simply don't put forth enough energy and intention to create substantial change. Instead, we get some good results, some bad results; or in extreme cases, no results at all.

As Robert Collier proposes, if we just keep working at it day in and day out – in other words being very consistent, even in small doses – we begin to see more stable results. The more regularly we do something, the easier it gets to keep doing it daily. So, rather than trying to change your financial picture in one fell swoop, you may want to instead focus on taking many small steps day after day. This will make your journey seem less strenuous, while also yielding results more frequently, which will strengthen your motivation to keep working at it consistently.

Affirmation:

Every small step brings me closer to success and financial abundance.

Day 129

The thing always happens that you really believe in;
and the belief in a thing makes it happen.

- Frank Loyd Wright

Since your beliefs usually work below your conscious level of awareness, you may not always notice when they are hindering your progress. The most obvious sign is when you are doing all the right things but still not getting results – even after months of trying. One of the simplest ways to begin transforming your beliefs is to make a list of statements that you would like to be true for you. For example, "I am abundant; I am confident; I have plenty of money; I am successful."

As you read these statements to yourself, notice that you probably feel an inner twinge of doubt or disbelief; in other words, they do not feel "true" to you. Now, adjust each statement so that it feels more believable to you. For example: "I am attracting more abundance every day; I choose to feel confident now; I love the feeling of having plenty of money." Reciting these modified statements should feel a little easier, and consistent repetition will make them feel truer as time goes on. Even better, your results will begin to show the difference.

Affirmation:

My beliefs are simply repetitive thoughts, and I can choose the thoughts I want to repeat.

Day 130

A failure is a man who has blundered, but is not able to cash in on the experience.

- Elbert Hubbard

None of us enjoy feeling like we have failed at something, especially if it's something we really wanted to achieve. However, what we do with the experience of failure says much more about our character and resilience than the failure itself does. Believe it or not, you can use past failures as stepping stones to greater things with a little shift in attitude about them. Start by making a list of your biggest failures from the past. Write about the time you were passed over for a promotion; didn't lose the weight you vowed to lose; or gave up on an important goal.

Now, for every failure you have listed, come up with one valuable lesson you learned from the experience. Make sure the lesson has positive benefits in some form, or even an insight that you can use in future situations. Then spend some time feeling genuinely grateful for these lessons or insights. When you do this often, you begin to see failures as valuable growing experiences that you can then apply to all future endeavors. More importantly, you begin to see yourself in a better light – not as a "failure" but as a person who learns and grows from every experience.

Affirmation:

I become better and stronger with every failure.

Day 131

Failures do what is tension relieving, while winners do what is goal achieving.

- Dennis Waitley

Have you ever given up on a goal because you were getting too stressed or frustrated to continue working on it? As Dennis Waitley suggests, sometimes we invite failure – even subconsciously – because we can't stand feeling strained or pressured. However, what many of us forget is that we don't have to give up on our goals to release tension; we simply have to approach them with a different attitude.

Most strain and stress occurs when we become too rigid in our thinking. We believe we must accomplish this or that in a given timeframe, or we must bring about this exact result in order to stay on track. However, rarely is this true. In fact, we usually find that if we relax our focus and be a bit more flexible in our approach, circumstances have a way of shifting around to make our progress faster and easier. Then we win by relieving tension AND achieving our goals.

Affirmation:

I am calm, relaxed and flexible when it comes to my goals and dreams.

Day 132

I cannot give you the formula for success, but I can give you the formula for failure - which is: Try to please everybody.

- Herbert Bayard Swope

Do you ever feel like you are "walking on eggshells" in your daily interactions with other people? Do you often worry about what people think about you and your activities, goals or dreams? As you may have already realized, trying to keep everyone around you happy is impossible because they all expect different things from you. But did you also know that trying to please everyone can block your attempts to receive greater abundance?

When you are worried about trying to keep other people happy, you are focused on fearful thoughts – the displeasure or anger they will direct your way if they don't get what they want. Unfortunately, fear is one of those emotions that are energetically in opposition to abundance, so by focusing on fear you end up blocking abundance. The solution is obvious: spend more time focusing intently on what YOU want, not worrying about what other people don't want. Your own happiness is your responsibility; other people's happiness is theirs

Affirmation:

I create my own happiness and I allow others to do the same for themselves.

Day 133

Success does not consist in never making blunders,
but in never making the same one a second time.

- Josh Billings

Do you have any situations in your life in which you seem to be hopelessly stuck? For example, is your financial situation still not improving despite months of consistent effort on your part; are your relationships still distant or troubled; are you struggling with a persistent health challenge? With long-standing issues like these, it's important to spend some time reviewing them and reflecting on the possibility that you may be making the same mistakes over and over again – therefore blocking your desired outcome from manifesting.

Attracting anything into your life requires a few deliberate steps: getting very clear about what you want, knowing that you deserve to have it, letting go so the universe can start forming it, moving yourself into alignment to receive it, and staying alert for inspired actions that may come your way. Examining your thoughts, feelings and actions over the past few months may reveal that you weren't completing each step fully which only keeps your desire hanging in limbo. If you adjust your approach slightly in these areas, you should notice the blockage start to loosen.

Affirmation:

I receive valuable insights by monitoring my progress.

Day 134

The secret of success in life is for a man to be ready for his opportunity when it comes.

- Earl of Beaconsfield

Being prepared to take advantage of opportunities can often make the difference between success and failure. Likewise, it can also pay great dividends to be prepared to receive great abundance when it arrives. You may think you are already prepared to receive it, but consider these points: Do you tend to give more attention to the things that are going wrong in your life, rather than the things that are going right? Do you focus more on what you don't have than what you do have? Do you often feel resentful of people who appear to have more money than you?

Habits like these will keep you out of alignment with great wealth because you are focused on the perception of "not having enough". To turn this around, simply begin training your mind to find the nugget of abundance (i.e. goodness) in every situation, and to feel glad about it. Be genuinely happy for people who seem to be doing well financially. Be grateful for the good things that come your way – even if there are also not-so-good things in the mix. The more you do this, the more you are preparing your mind to receive the abundance you are asking for.

Affirmation:

I see abundance everywhere I look.

Day 135

If you wish success in life, make perseverance your bosom friend, experience your wise counselor, caution your elder brother, and hope your guardian genius.

- Joseph Addison

When it comes to attracting wealth into your life, you probably already know that there is much more to the process than merely "thinking about" wealth. In the quote above, Joseph Addison offers some great advice for pursuing your goals and dreams and creating a successful life. These same suggestions will work well on your wealth attraction efforts too, if you understand how to apply them.

Perseverance will be required as you learn how to permanently shift your focus from lack to abundance, and putting forth the effort in the beginning will continue to pay off for the rest of your life. Experience can teach you a lot about yourself and help make your future efforts go more smoothly. Proceeding cautiously, one step at a time, can help you avoid taking on more than you can handle, and finally hope helps you expand your mind and be open to the many possibilities available to you.

Affirmation:

Success is a journey of gradual mastery.

Day 136

Impatience never commanded success.

- Edwin H. Chapin

When it comes to the Law of Attraction, impatience is like a big blockage tossed into your energetic frequency. It may not always be easy to wait patiently, especially when you really need something to come quickly – but it's important to understand what is happening with your energetic signal when you try to hurry it along. As you hop around feeling anxious and frustrated that something you want hasn't yet arrived, here is what the universe hears:

"I don't have this thing I need, and I need it really badly. I am requesting more and more experiences where I don't have what I need. I am requesting more and more experiences where I feel frustrated and unfulfilled." To avoid sending messages like this, try repeating something like this: "I know it will arrive with perfect timing. I know it's already mine. I know I already have everything I need." As you do this, the universe will pick up on your certainty and contentment and then send experiences and outcomes that will reflect that energy.

Affirmation:

Everything happens with perfect timing when I expect it.

Day 137

The talent of success is nothing more than doing what you can do, well.

- Henry W. Longfellow

Contrary to traditional goal-setting methods, working with the Law of Attraction can be very liberating in the sense that you do not have to know how you are going to accomplish every phase of your goal. You don't have to know how or when or where everything will come together. In fact, if you try to figure it all out and do everything yourself, you will likely end up causing delays and obstacles with your interference.

If you instead form a picture of the completed end result you desire, keep infusing it with energy and intention, and then allow the universe to start putting it together, you will be led to exactly the right opportunities to make it happen. However, be aware that you still may not get the full picture right away. Instead, you will be led to the next step. Once you complete that step, you will be led to the next, and so on until finally you arrive at your destination. Simply let go, trust that it will all unfold perfectly, and keep putting one foot in front of the other.

Affirmation:

I am ready to take the next step, and that's all I need to do.

Day 138

To climb steep hills requires a slow pace at first.

- Shakespeare

Transforming your thoughts and beliefs can definitely feel like climbing a steep hill because of the effort required. When you are climbing a steep hill and you stop walking, what happens? You stop making progress. The same thing happens if you aren't consistent and persistent enough with your visualization and meditation sessions, or any other technique you choose to use to manifest wealth. And at the beginning, it definitely seems like you're moving very slowly.

However, as you keep working on it day after day, you finally crest the top of the hill and every step after that becomes much easier. In fact, you can even afford to coast now and then because you have made so much progress and built so much momentum that it will continue to carry you along. Keeping this analogy in mind when you find that you are struggling to stay focused or committed can serve as a powerful reminder that it won't always be so difficult – if you can be patient through the rough spots, you will be coasting before you know It.

Affirmation:

I choose to be consistent with my efforts.

Day 139

A happy life consists not in the absence, but in the mastery of hardships.

- Helen Keller

One of the more common misconceptions about the Law of Attraction is that once you know how to use it, your life will run like a well-oiled machine; all problems will vanish and everything will be perfect, orderly and harmonious. Most often it doesn't work out that way. Challenges and upheavals will still happen. Occasionally you may be surprised by an event you didn't expect. You may still be disappointed when something doesn't work out the way you hoped, and other people may not always act in ways you appreciate.

The true gift in deliberately using the Law of Attraction is that you can make these upheavals less frequent and intense than they would otherwise be. Instead of reacting emotionally to challenges and fueling them, you can calmly assess situations, choose better outcomes and then direct your intention toward them. Even better, you will be able to call forth a higher frequency of "good" experiences to balance out the challenges. Your life may not run like a well-oiled machine, but it will be clear that you are never powerless and you always have choices.

Affirmation:

I choose to transform challenges into positive experiences.

Day 140

Far better is it to dare mighty things, to win glorious triumphs, even though checkered by failure...than to rank with those poor spirits who neither enjoy much nor suffer much, because they live in a gray twilight that knows not victory nor defeat.

- Theodore Roosevelt

Living a dull, mundane existence is one of the side effects that come from not knowing that you have the power to create the life of your dreams. When you truly know that you have the ability to choose your life circumstances, you feel inspired and passionate about the many options open to you. You feel eager to stretch your limits, take bigger risks and achieve bigger goals – simply because you can.

The same concept applies to your finances. If you settle for having only so much money because it's all you think you can achieve, the universe will not challenge that belief; it will simply deliver what you expect to have. Likewise if you place limits on the ways that money can come to you, money can only come in those ways. One of the most empowering beliefs you can begin to foster within yourself is that the universe can find endless ways to deliver what you ask for, so it's a good idea to ask for as much as you really want and be eager to receive it.

Affirmation:

I continuously expand my vision of great abundance.

Day 141

Let us strive on to finish the work we are in...

- Abraham Lincoln

Giving up too soon is one of the biggest mistakes that many people make when working with the Law of Attraction. It's important to remember that you have to build up a good amount of energy and intention and allow for a period of gestation before you will receive what you want. This is not because the universe can't deliver it immediately, but more often because you are not in alignment with receiving it when you first conceive the desire.

The good news is that every time you work on expanding your beliefs, every time you affirm your worthiness, and every time you expect good things to happen, you move one step closer to being able to receive the things you are attracting. And while this transition is happening, you must take care not to keep checking to see if those things have arrived yet – just like you would never dig up seeds from the ground to see if they are starting to blossom into life.

Affirmation:

Every day I come into closer alignment with my dreams.

Day 142

The question should be, is it worth trying to do, not can it be done.

- Allard Lowenstein

Have you ever set an intention to have something and when it arrived you weren't pleased by it? Most often this happens because you weren't clear on what you really wanted – only what you thought you wanted. For example, you may have believed that having a certain sum of money would make you feel abundant, but months later when you actually did receive it you realized you didn't feel any different than you did before. In fact, you may have then set your sights on an even larger sum of money, since the smaller sum didn't satisfy you.

A good way to avoid this problem in the future is to focus on the essence of the feeling you want, and not worry so much about the specific ways the feeling can be achieved. If your desire is to feel very secure and wealthy so that you would never have to worry about money again, start practicing that feeling now. Then the universe will automatically begin forming situations and resources to perfectly support that feeling – and every manifestation will be satisfying.

Affirmation:

My feelings communicate the essence of my desire.

Day 143

It was a high counsel that I once heard given to a young person, "Always do what you are afraid to do."

- Ralph Waldo Emerson

Feeling fearful about an aspect of your goals is one of the most common ways you can block the abundance you desire. Even though you may want something badly, if there is even one tiny piece of it that makes you feel uncomfortable, you will not allow it into your experience. For example, if you were trying to attract a sum of money that was much larger than the level of abundance you have now, you may feel a bit intimidated about actually handling so much money. This hesitation is noted by the universe and the delivery of money is held back.

One of the best ways to get around this fear is to start practicing having the money (or whatever else intimidates you) daily. Imagine as much detail as you can; see yourself managing the money and feeling completely comfortable as you do so. Mentally run through this scene and any others that make you feel nervous as often as you can. The more effectively you can convince your subconscious mind that there is nothing to fear, the quicker it will relax and release the resistance.

Affirmation:

I release feelings of intimidation and replace them with confidence.

Day 144

If you do not hope, you will not find what is beyond your hopes.

- St. Clement of Alexandra

Hope can be a powerful part of your attraction routine, but only if you use it in a proactive way. When most people "hope," they are actually doubting. They hope it doesn't rain, while glancing worriedly at the sky. They hope traffic isn't too bad on the way to work, and of course they usually run into a few delays. When it comes to the Law of Attraction, hoping needs to be a bit more forceful and targeted than these examples.

Hoping is actually planning. Whatever you hope does – or doesn't – happen is the very outcome you are infusing with your intention. Rather than hoping it doesn't rain, try hoping that it will be a gorgeous, sunny day. Rather than hoping traffic isn't too bad, try hoping that your ride will be smooth, speedy and safe. Rather than hoping you have enough money, try hoping that you can find enough ways to spend your ever-growing abundance. You will be able to feel a noticeable difference in the energy you are emitting toward these more positive intentions.

Affirmation:

I always hope for the outcome I want to experience.

Day 145

We are all inventors, each sailing out on a voyage of discovery, guided each by a private chart, of which there is no duplicate. The world is all gates, all opportunities.

– Ralph Waldo Emerson

Ralph Waldo Emerson's inspiring words serve as a great reminder that we are each "inventing" our reality in every moment. That means that no matter where we believe we may have gone wrong in the past, no matter how far we may have gone off-course with our plans, we can simply choose a brand new destination, set our sails and begin moving in that direction. And best of all, we can do this as many times as we like. If we get to one destination and decide we don't like it, we can immediately head for another.

As he says, "the world is all gates, all opportunities" – which means we can turn any situation into a better one simply by being open to the possibilities. If you haven't yet been viewing your life in this way, start today! Start by opening your mind to the wonders around you; by imagining how exciting your life can become if you simply start moving in different directions; and by trusting that there are never any mistakes, failures or unsolvable problems.

Affirmation:

I am creating a magnificent future right now.

Day 146

Knowing is not enough; we must apply. Willing is not enough; we must do.

- Johann Wolfgang von Goethe

Have you ever received a nudge from the universe to take action but held back because you felt uncertain about it? You may have heard that inspired actions will always feel easy and enjoyable when you take them, and this is true. What you may not realize is that these opportunities may seem frightening when they first appear before you. Not because the actions themselves seem intimidating, but you may worry that they are not inspired actions at all; only wishful thinking – and nothing good will come from them.

The thing to remember in moments like these is that no action is ever wasted effort. In fact, you can stack the odds in your favor if you do two important things. First, specifically intend that something positive will come from the action(s) you are about to take. Second, be completely detached from how and when those good results will appear. This will keep your expectations high and your mind open to recognize even unexpected opportunities that may arise.

Affirmation:

I take action for the fun of it and expect the best possible outcome.

Day 147

Nothing great was ever achieved without enthusiasm.

- Ralph Waldo Emerson

It's hard to deny the true power of enthusiasm, especially where the Law of Attraction is concerned. Have you ever woken up in a great mood and had a truly fantastic day? It wasn't just that you had a great day because you were in a great mood – your mood itself actually attracted corresponding experiences. This concept works extremely well in the attraction of abundance too; the more enthusiastic and excited you are about abundance, the more abundance you will attract into your life.

Here's a fun way to prove this to yourself: In the morning when you first wake up, spend 5 or 10 minutes thinking about abundance and becoming very excited about it. You can imagine having lots of money in the bank, or spending big sums of money on a shopping spree, or any other scenario that pumps up your positive emotions. Then keep this enthusiastic mindset strong for the rest of the day and notice how many expressions of abundance are drawn to you. Even if you don't see big results the first day, try it again because the more you do it the better it works.

Affirmation:

My enthusiasm attracts abundance quickly into my life.

Day 148

Don't find fault, find a remedy.

- Henry Ford

Henry Ford's suggestion provides a great analogy for the way many people use the Law of Attraction in their lives. They spend 15 to 30 minutes a day focusing on the things they want, and the rest of their time complaining and feeling frustrated about the many things they don't want. Do you do this too? Unfortunately, this amounts to finding fault rather than finding a remedy. Even though it's perfectly natural to feel frustrated when things around you are unpleasant, this type of mindset can only keep attracting more of what you don't want.

As difficult as it may seem at first, you have to put your full effort into focusing on what you do want, rather than what you don't. When something goes wrong, you have a choice whether to complain about it, or intend something better; to get angry about it, or focus on a peaceful solution. What you choose to do in the heat of the moment is what will ultimately determine the progress you make as you consciously create your life.

Affirmation:

It's easy to direct my focus to something I want.

Day 149

Go confidently in the direction of your dreams. Live the life you have imagined.

- Henry David Thoreau

This famous suggestion by Henry David Thoreau seems easy enough at first glance – until we actually try to put it into action. "Going confidently" in the direction of our dreams can feel like an impossible challenge without a strong belief in our own abilities. Instead, most of us tend to creep, shuffle and tiptoe in the direction of our dreams – ready to backpedal quickly if we sense the first hint of anxiety or fear come over us.

What we often forget is that much of our inner confidence comes from consistently doing the things we fear and realizing that they weren't so bad after all. If you currently find yourself standing on the brink between wanting to pursue a goal and feeling overwhelmed by uncertainty that you have what it takes to succeed, perhaps a better approach might be to "Go hopefully" in the direction of your dreams – trusting that the universe will be there to back you up and believing that you will develop stronger confidence as you keep moving forward

Affirmation:

Hope, trust and action build my confidence.

Day 150

The greatest gift you can give another is the purity of your attention.

- Richard Moss

Do you consider yourself to be a good listener? Would you say that you have a strong ability to stay focused? You probably know that both of these skills must be developed over time with consistent effort, but you may not immediately realize the power they hold when it comes to money and wealth. Richard Moss says that purity of attention is a great gift you can give to others, but you can also give the same gift to yourself by training your mind to harness your creative power and direct it where you want it to go.

Many of us today have fairly undisciplined minds; moving through our days on autopilot and rarely flexing our "focus muscles". As a result, our ability to consciously direct our thoughts gets weaker and weaker, which results in a mixture of wanted and unwanted manifestations in our lives. If this has been a problem for you, turning it around is as easy as practicing your ability to focus for a few minutes each day. The more you do it the easier it gets, and the easier it gets the more effective you become at deliberately drawing abundance into your life.

Affirmation:

Every day my focus on abundance grows stronger.

Day 151

Those who wish to sing, always find a song.

- Swedish Proverb

This proverb shares a great example about the power of your thoughts to easily attract the resources you need to achieve your deepest heart's desires. As you focus consistently on something you want while staying in a positive, hopeful, enthusiastic mindset, you are putting into motion a flurry of energetic forces that begin shifting physical reality as you know it. The resources, people, funds, opportunities, creative inspiration, and time that will be required to bring this desire into being begin flowing immediately in your direction.

However, because we can't see this energetic shifting at first, we get frustrated when it seems like nothing is happening – and that stops the energetic progress in its tracks. To prevent this from happening with your desire, make it your mission to keep an attitude of hope, joy and faith, even if progress seems slow. Keep busy with activities that make you feel inspired and passionate. By doing so, you will be keeping the door open for their arrival.

Affirmation:

My consistent belief is a magnet for the resources I need.

Day 152

Our greatest glory is not in never failing, but in rising up every time we fail.

- Ralph Waldo Emerson

One of the reasons we often give up on our dreams and goals is because we associate our success with the achievement of a specific outcome. If the outcome we want seems slow in coming, we start to fear that it will never happen – which means that all of our actions will have been in vain. However, there is a simple way to bypass this frustration, and that is by choosing to see our daily efforts as their own rewards.

A good way to start is by reinforcing the positive benefits of the actions you take each day. You might say to yourself, "I'm going to take this action because it will be fun." Or, "Taking this action makes me feel productive, like I'm co-creating with the universe." Or, "Even if nothing comes from this action right away, I'm going to do it anyway." When you keep focusing on the satisfaction you get from taking action toward something you want, you automatically start enjoying the journey rather than rushing blindly toward the finish line.

Affirmation:

I gain something good from every step I take

Day 153

*Look within. Within is the fountain of good, and it will
ever bubble up, if thou wilt ever dig.*

- Marcus Aurelius

One of the most challenging truths to grasp about the
attraction of wealth is that it all comes from within us.
Many of us have spent years "pursuing" abundance
through purely physical actions, which limits the
success we can achieve because we only have so
many hours in a day and can only accomplish so
much in that length of time. However, when we finally
begin to see evidence that our outer level of wealth
grows in direct proportion to our inner development,
we open the door to truly unlimited abundance.

Finally we understand that our thoughts form the
basis for everything we experience. Finally we
understand that only our limiting beliefs can prevent
us from achieving our goals. With these realizations
comes a much easier, playful approach to life. Rather
than pursuing wealth, we learn how to open our
hearts to joy and allow wealth to flow effortlessly into
our lives. Rather than trying to force things to happen
outwardly, we surrender to the present moment and
believe that things will just keep getting better and
better. And because we believe it, they do.

Affirmation:

I relax and open to the flow of abundance within me.

Day 154

We are what we repeatedly do. Excellence, then, is not an act, but a habit.

- Aristotle

Aristotle's famous words have a powerful meaning when viewed in context with the Law of Attraction: Not only are we what we repeatedly do, we are what we repeatedly "vibrate" – as in the energetic signal we send according to our thoughts and feelings. Do you frequently vibrate feelings of frustration or fear about your current financial situation? Do you keep feeling impatient that your abundance hasn't yet shown up? The irony is that you cannot change your circumstances until you adjust the content of your signal.

To attract abundance, you must vibrate as if you already have abundance. To attract financial security, you must vibrate as if you already feel secure. Rather than trying to get to a better place, you need to think, feel and act as if you are already in that better place. It may not always be easy but if you strive to make it a daily habit, eventually you will begin to vibrate differently and experience different results.

Affirmation:

I vibrate whatever I focus my attention upon.

Day 155

Until you are happy with who you are, you will never be happy with what you have.

- Zig Ziglar

Zig Ziglar shares a great insight about the power of being the person who will attract the lifestyle you want to live. Most of us approach this process backwards: we try to "get" the things we want so we can then "be" the person who has those things. A fun exercise to turn this around is to practice daily being the person who already has the things you want. For example, if you want to have millions of dollars in the bank, practice being a multi-millionaire.

Ask yourself in every moment, "How would a multi-millionaire think, speak and act in this situation?" Then do your best to think, speak and act in just that way. In the back of your mind you will be well aware that you're just "pretending" – but it won't matter because you will still be infusing your intention to be a multi-millionaire into everything you do. The universe will receive that signal every time you do it, and over time your financial resources will begin to grow and multiply.

Affirmation:

I am now the person I always dreamed of becoming.

Day 156

Cherish your visions and your dreams as they are the children of your soul, the blueprints of your ultimate achievements.

- Napoleon Hill

When dreams are first born, they are as delicate and fragile as newborn babies. It is only after they have been infused with loving, nurturing energy and given time to expand that they are strong enough to take on life of their own. For this reason, you will want to be careful about sharing your dreams with others when they are still fresh, new and tender. Just as you wouldn't hand over your newborn child to an untrustworthy person, you shouldn't expose your dreams to critical, closed-minded people.

Most often when you feel the urge to share your dream with others, you are seeking confirmation that your idea is a good one. Unfortunately, not everyone will agree that it is, and if your own confidence in your dreams is shaky, their negativity may be enough to deflate your enthusiasm. A wiser move is to keep your dreams close to your heart, think about them often, and give them time to develop energetic substance. Your confidence will continue to strengthen and expand – and eventually you'll find that the opinions of others simply don't matter to you anymore

Affirmation:

I protect and nurture my dreams into their full brilliance.

Day 157

Obstacles are necessary for success because…victory comes only after many struggles and countless defeats.

- Og Mandino

Og Mandino shares an interesting insight about the value of obstacles, but it's important that we clarify the difference between overcoming obstacles and unnecessarily struggling. Obstacles are a natural part of any endeavor, and all they mean is that the time isn't quite right for this phase of the plan to proceed. Perhaps conditions necessary for the next phase of the plan aren't quite in place yet, or maybe we still have a bit of resistance within ourselves that needs to be cleared.

Struggle, on the other hand, is what happens when we try to force our way forward even when things don't seem to be flowing easily. For example, when we encounter an obstacle, our frustration may cause us to make hasty decisions that only cause more problems and delays. A good way to avoid this is by turning within and getting clear on why the obstacle has shown up – and then surrendering to our inner wisdom about the right approach to the problem. This allows us to see the obstacle as a momentary pause rather than an immovable roadblock.

Affirmation:

I trust my inner wisdom to guide me around all obstacles.

Day 158

If you want to reach a goal, you must 'see the reaching' in your own mind before you actually arrive at your goal.

- Zig Ziglar

Zig Ziglar's intriguing words remind us that there is great power in striving to do, be and have more in our lives. When put in context with the Law of Attraction, this concept could also be described as "seeing the expansion" of our own potential. We do this naturally as we visualize our goals and dreams – but then we revert right back to our present state when going about our daily activities. We are so accustomed to seeing ourselves as average people with average lives that we forget that we are capable of so much more.

One good way to overcome this mundane outlook in your own life is by consistently affirming that you have endless possibilities for growth and expansion. You might start with affirmations like these: "I am always evolving and expanding into a more powerful person; I have unlimited potential to be whoever I want to be; There are no limits to the things I can achieve." The more you reinforce your own limitless nature, the more easily you will be able to "see the reaching" toward anything you desire.

Affirmation:

I am truly limitless in every way.

Day 159

Words of love are works of love.

- William Alger

This great quote by William Alger reminds us that the essence of our intention is infused into everything we do – and that very essence is what will be reflected back to us in the form of corresponding results and experiences. When you think about this concept in relation to abundance, it becomes clear that one of the best ways to attract more money into your life is to speak only of abundance, think only of abundance, and act only in accordance with abundance.

Just as you wouldn't pop a mud-pie into the oven and expect to see a chocolate cake emerge, you can't infuse your actions with thoughts of lack and scarcity and expect to see abundance emerge. Granted, it can be challenging to think and speak only of abundance when all you see around you is lack and struggle – so you may want to try reciting this simple statement over and over: "I choose to see abundance everywhere I look." Before long you will begin to recognize the great abundance surrounding you, and the more you focus on it the more it will multiply in your life.

Affirmation:

I infuse my every thought, word and action with the essence of abundance.

Day 160

Let others lead small lives, but not you. Let others argue over small things, but not you. Let others cry over small hurts, but not you. Let others leave their future in someone else's hands, but not you.

- Jim Rohn

One of the reasons we often hold back on creating positive changes in our lives is because we struggle with a keen sense of powerlessness. We may labor under difficult financial constraints and have no idea how to turn them around; or we may remain locked in painful relationships for years and feel hesitant to release them. Once we learn about the power of our minds to alter our physical surroundings, we feel a ray of hope that maybe we can begin moving slowly toward a brighter tomorrow.

Rather than feeling pressured by the thought of taking drastic action to improve our lives, we can instead begin simply pondering the changes we'd like to make, then slowly forming a mental picture of what a better outcome might look like – and as these visions begin to take form, we will eventually be inspired to take action to fulfill the dream. Through this inner transition, we turn our powerlessness into a welcome state of empowerment. No longer are we locked into leading "small lives" – we can joyfully embrace a deeper, more purposeful state of being.

Affirmation:

I am empowered and inspired by my inner vision.

Day 161

The ultimate measure of a man is not where he stands in moments of comfort and convenience, but where he stands at times of challenge and controversy.

- Martin Luther King Jr.

Deliberately creating your life can be eye-opening because as you learn to master your thoughts you will be faced with many opportunities to put your newfound knowledge into practice. When difficult or unpleasant experiences arise, you may find yourself automatically responding from your old, limited mindset rather than the relaxed, expanded mindset you have been painstakingly developing. During these moments of frustration you may mistakenly believe that you haven't made any progress and must be doing something "wrong".

Experiences like these do not mean you are doing anything wrong – nor do they mean that you haven't made any progress. They simply reveal the need for further practice. Changing your default mindset is not an instant process. You will need to work consistently at it every day for weeks or even months, and progress may seem slow at times. At first you may seem to have more control over your thoughts during calm periods, but eventually your control during more turbulent experiences will become apparent too.

Affirmation:

My focus grows stronger and more positive every day.

Day 162

Love is like a friendship caught on fire. In the beginning a flame, very pretty, often hot and fierce, but still only light and flickering. As love grows older, our hearts mature and our love becomes as coals, deep-burning and unquenchable.

- Bruce Lee

Bruce Lee's description of love offers a great analogy for the process of coming into our own creative power. When we first learn about the Law of Attraction, it seems so exciting and new that we can't wait to begin applying it to every aspect of our lives. And yes, we can certainly accomplish a lot with such passion and enthusiasm. However, we quickly discover that we cannot keep up that intense pace for long. Not only does it require a lot of our energy, we also begin to lose interest if we don't start seeing results from our efforts immediately.

For those of us who truly "get it," however, we won't give up at this point. Instead, we begin to settle into a deeper, more meaningful application of the principles. Rather than trying to change everything in our lives overnight, we begin seeing our mastery of the Law of Attraction as a fulfilling journey that unfolds for the rest of our lives. With this awareness comes the realization that we have plenty of time to achieve our dreams, so there's no reason not to relax and enjoy the ride.

Affirmation:

I allow my creative power to emerge slowly and steadfastly

Day 163

You cannot control what happens to you, but you can control your attitude toward what happens to you, and in that, you will be mastering change rather than allowing it to master you.

- Brian Tracy

Developing a flexible, confident state of mind is one of the greatest benefits that come from deliberately improving your thoughts. Flexibility and confidence are important qualities to have because they give you the power of resilience, no matter what may happen around you. Knowing that the Law of Attraction responds to your mental and emotional state by returning corresponding experiences, you can easily see that your day to day activities would be generally positive if you are calm and centered.

Even when unexpected events pop up, you would have the emotional fortitude to handle them calmly and efficiently, rather than reacting with outbursts of fear or anger. Developing this emotional fortitude is as simple as getting into the habit of staying calm no matter what happens in your life. Try repeating this several times a day: "I choose to remain calm and centered today." If upsetting events occur, take an emotional step back and repeat that line again and you should feel your frustration dissipate, allowing an opportunity to handle the situation calmly.

Affirmation:

A calm mind creates a harmonious environment.

Day 164

All men dream but not equally. Those who dream by night in the dusty recesses of their minds wake in the day to find that it was vanity; but the dreamers of the day are dangerous men, for they may act their dream with open eyes to make it possible.

- T.E. Lawrence

All dreams are conceived in the fleeting, ephemeral realm of thoughts, and through your physical actions they are born into physical reality. Usually this is a gradual process of moving steadily forward, taking decisive action and waiting patiently for your vision to become real. However, there is a way to begin cementing your dreams in the physical world before you even begin taking action toward them, and that is by writing them down in full detail and continuously expanding them.

Here's a fun way to begin. Get a new notebook and designate it as your "Dream Journal". Open to the first page and begin writing your vision for the way you would like your life to be. You can write about having plenty of income, winning the lottery, buying the home of your dreams, creating a successful new business, or anything you like. Spend time every day refining and clarifying these dreams, and before long you will notice that they are already starting to feel more real to you than they did when you were merely thinking about them.

Affirmation:

The more I clarify my dreams, the more tangible they become.

Day 165

A real decision is measured by the fact that you've taken a new action. If there's no action, you haven't truly decided.

- Tony Robbins

Have you ever avoided taking action to achieve a goal because you felt uncertain or nervous about it? Tony Robbins offers a great insight about the power of being committed and taking action to demonstrate that commitment. You already know that the Law of Attraction responds to your dominant thoughts, emotions and beliefs, but what you may not realize is that physical action can act as a "bridge" that links your mental and emotional energy to tangible physical results.

This is very different than trying to accomplish something with physical action alone, which often leaves you feeling frustrated and exhausted. Instead, if you focus on creating the right mind-set and also taking one or more small action steps toward something you want, you can speed up the rate at which your goal will be fulfilled. A clear desire, plus positive expectation, plus confident forward movement always equals a positive response from the universe.

Affirmation:

Moving forward demonstrates my commitment to my goals.

Day 166

I do not think much of a man who is not wiser today than he was yesterday.

- Abraham Lincoln

One aspect of wealth attraction that is rarely discussed is the inner journey you take as you grow in wisdom and confidence. As Abraham Lincoln suggests above, the true mark of success is a person who continues to grow and learn each day, regardless of the visible achievements he makes in the outer world. In fact, as you may realize by now you cannot achieve anything lasting on the outside without inner expansion taking place first.

Unfortunately, many people miss this important truth and attempt to compensate for their inner scarcity by making big outer achievements – but the Law of Attraction keeps returning them right back to circumstances that match their inner level of abundance. You can prevent this from happening to you by making sure that you are learning and growing every step of the way along your journey – rather than trying to create outer success to make yourself feel more successful within. When you work from the inside out, the journey to success becomes easy and fun!

Affirmation:

Every day I expand in wisdom and confidence.

Day 167

He who climbs above the cares of this world, and turns his face to his God, has found the sunny side of life.

- Spurgeon

One of the more challenging aspects of attracting abundance is learning how to turn away from negative perceptions and trust that the universe is working on your behalf. For example, how many times have you reacted angrily or fearfully to an unexpected expense? How many times have you lost hope and decided that your financial situation would never improve? These types of reactions only accomplish one thing: firmly rooting your perception in physical reality. Believe it or not, you do have another option.

When you get into the habit of proactively trusting that the universe is helping you with every situation, you begin investing your energy and intention into more productive outcomes. Next time you encounter a situation that could potentially have a negative outcome, deliberately tell the universe, "I know that you are working on this situation for me. I am letting go and trusting you to handle it; let me know if there is anything I can do to help." More often than not, you will be pleasantly surprised as events shift to your advantage in ways you couldn't have imagined.

Affirmation:

I put my full trust in the universe to help me in every possible way.

Day 168

Love is a game that two can play and both win.

- Eva Gabor

Envision the universe as a giant mirror that reflects the essence of whatever you project with your thoughts and feelings. Projecting feelings of love and kindness will result in love and kindness flowing back to you. The essence of anger and fear, sadness and despair, joy and gratitude will be reflected right back to you too. Not surprisingly, it works the same way with abundance – and it works whether your thoughts are directed toward yourself or others.

Every time you feel glad about someone else's success and abundance, you are attracting more success and abundance back to yourself. Every time you feel resentful about someone else's good fortune because yours isn't as grand, you are strengthening your perception of lack. Every time you feel glad about your own level of abundance – even if it's just a dollar in your pocket – you are projecting the belief "I am abundant, I love having money" and the universe must reflect more of that essence back to you.

Affirmation:

By projecting thoughts of abundance, I receive more abundance.

Day 169

In every tear is a seed of healing.

- Author Unknown

Inevitably as you work on drawing greater abundance into your life, you will enter periods of time where it seems as if you have reached a plateau that you cannot seem to get beyond no matter how hard you try. These stagnant periods are often caused by inner blockages that impede your progress until you clear them. One of the most effective ways to dissolve these blockages is to think of them as a form of "illness" that must be healed. For our purposes, we will define "illness" as an absence of positive, vital life energy flow.

When your physical body becomes un-well, the most common advice is to rest and allow time for the body to restore its energy and strength. Believe it or not, this same advice can work incredibly well with mental and emotional blockages. For a few days, set aside your goals and plans and focus only on taking it easy. Detach from the need to change anything and instead simply be happy now. When you do this, you create a space for "healing" to take place; the blockage dissolves and your strength and focus is restored.

Affirmation:

I allow myself the time and space to heal mentally, emotionally and physically.

Day 170

The hardest arithmetic to master is that which enables us to count our blessings.

- Eric Hoffer

You are probably familiar with the power of gratitude when it comes to attracting more abundance into your life, but you can apply this concept in more powerful ways than you may have done before. For example, you may know how to keep a "gratitude journal," which involves writing down five or more things that you are grateful for each day. You can record positive experiences you had during each day, list the blessings in your life such as family, friends, your job, and so on.

However, you can also turn your gratitude focus into an ongoing exercise every day. One good way to do this is by constantly trying to find one good thing to be grateful for in every situation. Feel grateful for an extra few minutes to collect your thoughts before a meeting; for the pleasant waiter who smiles and jokes as he serves your lunch; for an unexpected discount when buying something you need. Even better, include a solid reason why you are grateful for these things, because you will be acknowledging the positive impact these experiences have on your life.

Affirmation:

I can find endless things to be grateful for.

Day 171

We do not sing because we are happy, we are happy because we sing.

- William James

One of the most surprising ways that abundance can flow into your life is by purposely expressing feelings of happiness. Some people mistakenly believe that they must wait until they have abundance before they can feel happy, but the opposite is true when it comes to the Law of Attraction. When you feel genuinely happy, you have no inner resistance to the things you want to attract – including money and all forms of abundance. But how can you feel happy when things in your life are not the way you want them to be?

The fastest and easiest way to start is by finding just one thing that makes you feel happy when you think about it. It may be a person you love, a favorite hobby, or a simple affirmation like, "I love feeling happy." The more you think about things that make you feel happy, the more you communicate an intention to be happy to the universe, and the more the universe will return situations, people and events that do indeed make you feel happy – which will include money and other good things.

Affirmation:

When I feel happy, abundance flows easily to me.

Day 172

It is difficulties that show what men are.

– Epictetus

As you continue to grow in your ability to deliberately manifest abundance, you should notice that your emotional responses become calmer and more stable than they used to be – especially where negative situations are concerned. For example, a person who has truly mastered her thoughts will handle adversity calmly and confidently, while a person who is still stuck in a "victim" mind-set would become flustered, angry or fearful in the same situation.

Pay attention to your own emotional responses during moments of uncertainty or adversity, and you will be able to see clearly how far you have come. When things go wrong, unexpected bills come in, or it seems as if you aren't making progress, notice your reactions to these events. If you find that you are still reacting with negative emotions, you may want to practice saying an affirmative intention like this one: "Scarcity and adversity are illusions. I choose to focus on abundance and opportunity now." Over time, your emotional state will reflect this belief too.

Affirmation:

I can feel the abundance within me when I stay calm.

Day 173

There is nothing that wastes the body like worry, and one who has any faith in God should be ashamed to worry about anything whatsoever.

- Mahatma Gandhi

Mahatma Gandhi's wise words are a great reminder about the destructive power of worry, not only to our bodies but to our level of abundance too. Worry is one of the strongest expressions of lack because it is really like an intention to NOT receive the outcome you want. When you worry that you won't have enough money to pay your bills, you are really communicating to the universe, "I choose not to have enough money to pay the bills." Even though you do want to have enough money, the universe reflects what you are focusing on, which is not enough.

Stopping this destructive cycle in your life takes a bit of conscious determination, but even the smallest bit of effort should begin to multiply quickly. Start by refusing to worry, no matter how tempted you are to do it. Instead, affirm with conviction that a positive outcome will be yours. When you do this, you communicate a message to the universe that says, "I trust that this will work out fine" – and the universe must return a result that is indeed "fine," or even "great".

Affirmation:

I replace worry with strong trust and allow the best outcome possible.

Day 174

Don't hurry, don't worry. You're only here for a short visit. So be sure to stop and smell the flowers.

- Walter Hagen

When it comes to attracting abundance, a big problem arises when you get stressed or approach it too seriously. The true essence of abundance is completely opposite "negativity" in all its forms – which would include stress, pessimism, doubt, frustration, anger, and the like. Getting stressed or being too serious about attracting abundance only keeps pushing it away because the frequencies are so different.

On the other hand, when you take Walter Hagen's advice and stop to smell the flowers – abundance flows easily and naturally. One of the simplest and most effective ways to get abundance flowing to you is through daily meditation. Scientific studies have proven that regular meditation provides many physical and emotional health benefits, and one of them is helping you to feel more relaxed and happy. Feeling relaxed and happy is perfectly in alignment with the essence of abundance, so you begin drawing more of it into your life.

Affirmation:

Abundance comes to me easily when I feel good.

Day 175

The reason why worry kills more people than work is that more people worry than work.

- Robert Frost

Worry is one of the surest ways to block abundance from entering your life because as you focus on possible negative outcomes you are actually drawing them into your life. More importantly, you are also blocking better experiences (including abundance) from coming into your life. One of the easiest ways to nip worry in the bud is by taking notice of the worrisome thoughts when they start and proactively turning them around to something more positive.

For example, if you catch yourself thinking, "I'm not sure if I'll have enough money to cover everything this month..." stop immediately and say, "Actually, I intend that I do have enough money to cover all of my bills this month, and I intend that I actually have some money left over." This type of affirmation may not yield instant results but as you do it regularly you will gradually feel more confident and secure about your money, which begins to attract even more.

Affirmation:

I have the power to deliberately choose my thoughts.

Day 176

Celebrate your success and find humor in your failures. Don't take yourself so seriously. Loosen up and everyone around you will loosen up. Have fun and always show enthusiasm. When all else fails, put on a costume and sing a silly song.

- Sam Walton

Humor is one of the greatest ways to help ease financial strain and start drawing great abundance into your life. One of the most helpful ways to use humor is for distraction from negative thoughts. When you find yourself feeling anxious or annoyed about something relating to your finances, deliberately turn your focus away from the situation and instead focus on something that makes you laugh. Watch a half-hour comedy sitcom on television, or keep a stash of funny books or magazines handy.

The most challenging thing about this exercise is being willing to let go of the negative thoughts and purposely focus on something better. If you feel resistance to improving your mood, try affirming something like this: "Even though I don't want to feel better right now, I'm going to do it anyway. I may not feel like laughing right now, but I'm going to give myself this time to relax and feel better because I deserve It." Then follow through and let that positive energy flow.

Affirmation:

I give myself permission to feel good.

Day 177

I will keep a smile on my face and in my heart even when it hurts today.

- Og Mandino

Og Mandino's wise words share a great example of the power of choosing your mindset day to day. All of us have moments (or entire days) where we feel sad, upset, angry or desperate and it seems like nothing will ever get better. The best way to overcome days like those is to decide that we're going to make the best of them no matter what. This is not the same thing as denying our feelings – it's more about acknowledging that we don't feel so good right now but we're going to put a smile on our face and do what we can to be happy anyway.

Doing this has an awesome benefit: as we intend to feel better and at least make an attempt to be happy right now, the universe begins shifting our circumstances to allow little bits of joy and peace into our lives immediately. That doesn't mean all of our problems evaporate, but their intensity eases slightly so they seem more manageable and we are better able to make it through the rest of the day.

Affirmation:

I choose to smile inside and out today.

Day 178

He who laughs, lasts.

- Zig Ziglar

Zig Ziglar's insightful statement above shares such a powerful key to deliberate creation: the only thing that makes our journey seem easy or difficult is our own perception of it. If we believe that improving our financial situation is going to be difficult, turbulent and uncertain, that's what we're going to see every step of the journey. On the other hand, when we lighten up and decide that the journey to abundance is going to be smooth, fun and rewarding, it will be.

Have you ever felt that bringing more abundance into your life was hard, unpleasant or draining in any way? If so, try making it fun and joyful from this moment on. Each morning when you wake up, affirm that you are going to enjoy the day and all of the wonderful things that will come your way. Affirm that abundance will flow easily to you from many different sources. As you keep doing this daily, your perception gradually shifts so that you place a stronger focus on the fun and easy parts of wealth attraction, which makes the entire journey seem like a breeze.

Affirmation:

Attracting abundance is fun and easy!

Day 179

Love is my religion - I could die for it.

- John Keats

John Keats's statement above is quite powerful when you put it in context with abundance and the Law of Attraction. If you substitute the word "love" with "abundance" – consider whether the intensity of your beliefs are strong enough to "die for". As a figure of speech, "to die for" would mean something that you believe in so strongly that everything else pales in comparison to it. Many of us don't have that level of belief in abundance – but we do in lack and struggle.

Why is it important to have a rock-solid, unwavering belief in abundance? Because until you do, your ability to attract it will be lessened. Developing a strong belief in abundance is as simple as continually reinforcing your belief that you deserve it, you can have it, the universe wants you to have it, and you will not settle for having less than what you are capable of creating. This kind of belief does takes time to build, but eventually you will feel so strongly about it that you would certainly "die for it."

Affirmation:

I believe in my abundance.

Day 180

Worry, like a rocking chair will give you something to do, but it won't get you anywhere.

- Vance Havner

When most of us worry, it's because we are trying to solve a problem we are facing in the moment. For example, worrying that we don't have enough money, frantically brainstorming ways we could attract or earn more money, and so on. The problem with doing this is that it is never effective. Like Vince Havner says above, it simply won't get you anywhere. All you do is keep rehashing the same problem – and a solution cannot come from focusing on the problem. Solutions can come only by opening your mind to allow them in.

One of the best ways to do this is by asking the universe to guide you to a solution. The next time you feel overwhelmed by a problem, first write it down. For example, "I don't know how to increase my income." Below the problem, write: "I intend to receive the perfect solution to clear this blockage." Then quiet your mind, relax your body, and ask for guidance from the universe. Then give it some time and the solution will likely appear when you least expect it.

Affirmation:

The universe guides me to the perfect solutions.

Day 181

One problem with gazing too frequently into the past is that we may turn around to find the future has run out on us.

- Michael Cibenko

Gazing too frequently into the past can indeed limit our enjoyment of the present and future – but there are times when it can be extremely helpful, especially where our attraction efforts are concerned. If you want to try an illuminating exercise, take a look around at your current life circumstances and then consider what kind of thoughts and feelings you must have had in the past in order to create those conditions.

This is not for the purposes of blaming yourself or beating yourself up for your "mistakes". Instead, see it as a great exercise to better focus your thoughts from this moment on. Consider the experiences and events you would like to have in the near future, choose the thoughts and feelings that will attract them, and then make it your daily work to focus on those thoughts and feelings to the exclusion of all others.

Affirmation:

I continuously improve my manifesting ability.

Day 182

Tell me who you love, and I'll tell you who you are.

– Proverb

The above proverb refers to the love of another person, but the same concept can also be applied to "what" you love – like abundance and lack. One common problem that many people have in attracting more abundance is that they have become a person who identifies with financial struggle and lack. Subconsciously they won't allow more abundance to flow into their lives because it would change who they believe themselves to be. Does this describe you?

If so, here is a powerful rule of thumb to remember: if you start changing who you are, your circumstances must change too. Changing who you are isn't as difficult as it may sound; it simply requires that you start thinking, feeling and acting like the person you want to become. For example, if you want to be a person to whom money flows easily, you start thinking, feeling and acting as if it does and little by little you should notice that you start feeling differently about money – and attracting more of it effortlessly.

Affirmation:

I can be whoever I want to be.

Day 183

You've got to sing like you don't need the money. You've got to love like you'll never get hurt. You've got to dance like there's nobody watching. You've got to come from the heart, if you want it to work.

- Susanna Clark

Susanna Clark's inspiring words reveal a key insight into the power of detachment. When it comes to the Law of Attraction, detachment is vital. Detachment means letting go – as opposed to trying to force things to happen in a certain way or timeframe. Whenever you're attached to a specific outcome you are restricting your energetic signal, which the Law of Attraction sees as a red light.

The best way to prevent this restriction is to simply relax and detach from needing things to be a certain way. Focus more of your attention on being happy now while also being optimistic that even greater things are coming your way soon. This can be challenging to do, but it becomes easier when you decide that you're going to trust that the universe is working on a perfect outcome in every situation. Just relax, let go, and enjoy this moment, and everything else will arrive with perfect timing.

Affirmation:

I am willing to relax and let my abundance flow.

Day 184

Happiness is beneficial for the body, but it is grief that develops the powers of the mind.

- Marcel Proust

While we are intensely focused on improving the quality of our thoughts and creating better circumstances, we sometimes forget to be thankful for our past challenges that have inspired us to make these changes. If not for our pain, struggle and dissatisfaction with various aspects of our lives, we would never be motivated to strive for better. We would simply stay in one place and experience less joy and abundance than we deserve.

Viewing your difficult experiences as training exercises that help you better clarify the things you want can help you see them in a new light. No longer will they be annoying situations that need to be removed, but rather welcome stepping stones to a better, brighter existence. And the more you focus on how every situation can be improved, the faster you begin to draw forth the resources and means to create ever-increasing levels of joy and abundance.

Affirmation:

Challenges help me become stronger and more focused.

Day 185

Some of God's greatest gifts are unanswered prayers.

- Garth Brooks

None of us likes to feel like our prayers (or intentions) are not being heard or answered by the universe, but Garth Brooks reminds us that sometimes this can actually be a good thing. The nature of our desires are so fleeting that we often think we want one thing, when we actually want something else entirely. Receiving what we think we want can block the arrival of what we really want and leave us feeling dissatisfied and unfulfilled.

Rather than being too specific with your prayers and intentions, you may want to try being more relaxed about them. Get clear about the true essence of what you want (for example, to be financially free and secure) and then ask the universe to show you the best way to achieve that goal. When you do this, you will quickly discover that there is no such thing as "unanswered prayers" – only great surprises as one desire after another is answered in inspiring ways.

Affirmation:

I allow the universe to surprise and delight me.

Day 186

The only cure for grief is action.

- George Henry Lewes

When it comes to the Law of Attraction, it's vital to first get your thoughts and emotions in alignment with the things you're trying to attract. However, pure physical action has great benefits also, one of which is making you feel like a co-creator with the universe. Rather than visualizing and sitting impatiently as you wait for your abundance to manifest, it can be much more rewarding to make a short list of action steps you can take to help get the ball rolling.

These action steps don't have to be overwhelming; in fact they can be very modest. But the more often you take deliberate action toward something you want, the more positive energy you will be directing toward the outcome. And when you combine these actions with right thinking and positive emotions like joy, excitement, enthusiasm and belief, the more the universe is going to be activated to return the best possible outcome.

Affirmation:

I am co-creating my abundance with the universe.

Day 187

It's not what happens to you, but how you react to it that matters.

- Epictetus

Have you ever had trouble controlling your spontaneous emotional reactions to the things that happen to you daily? When things go wrong do you react with anger, tears or hysteria? Very often this is the result of a build-up of frustration below your conscious awareness – until one little thing acts as "the straw that broke the camel's back" and you become extremely distressed even over minor issues.

Since the Law of Attraction sees these outbursts as "requests" for more upsetting situations, preventing them is a good idea. There is a way to neutralize feelings of frustration and stress before they ever reach the point of explosion; simply pay attention to your feelings throughout the day and take steps to quiet your mind and calm your emotions when you start to feel upset. Do this little by little all day long and gradually you will become the master of your thoughts and emotions, making those emotional outbursts extinct.

Affirmation:

I choose to feel calm and centered.

Day 188

Love looks not with the eyes, but with the mind.

– Shakespeare

William Shakespeare's famous words also fit well with learning to use the Law of Attraction in our lives, because we need to avoid looking at our life circumstances with our eyes and instead use our minds to "see" the reality we want to experience. Doing this requires a commitment to turn our attention away from situations that we don't want to replicate, and instead focus intently on the things we do want to create in our lives.

The biggest challenge with this objective is that it takes a lot of practice before we master it. We have been trained to think very logically about our lives and the conditions and events we see around us seem to be very real and solid. It is only when we remember that we are seeing a constantly shifting "reflection" of the essence of our thoughts and feelings that we understand we can take greater control by deliberately changing our thoughts to focus on better options.

Affirmation:

I choose to "see" only abundance and joy in my life.

Day 189

Work and play are words used to describe the same thing under differing conditions.

- Mark Twain

Most of us see work and play in entirely different ways – one is drudgery, the other is fun; one is unpleasant and boring, the other is inspiring and satisfying. However, Mark Twain's wise words remind us that work and play don't have to be so different. In fact, with a tiny shift in attitude work can become as enjoyable as play. To start, consider the key elements that make play so much fun.

One of the major benefits is that you want to do it. You look forward to the activity because you know it will be enjoyable, satisfying or rewarding in some way. In other words, there is a payoff that you will receive from the activity. If you approach your work in the opposite fashion by expecting it to be boring or unpleasant, it probably will be. But what might happen if you started expecting your work to be enjoyable and satisfying?

Affirmation:

I can find many reasons to enjoy my work.

Day 190

The desire of knowledge, like the thirst for riches, increases ever with the acquisition of it.

- Laurence Sterne

Have you ever thought that it will be nice when you finally know all there is to know about the Law of Attraction and you will have finally "mastered" it once and for all? While it's true that you can become very proficient in deliberate creation, you probably won't experience that sense of completion you may be hoping for. The reason is simple – there will always be more to learn no matter how much you know.

Whether the knowledge you seek pertains to the Law of Attraction, other universal laws, other techniques and methods to train your mind or anything else, you (like everyone else) will probably always have a thirst for new knowledge, new insight and new wisdom. And this is a great thing because there are truly no limits to how much knowledge you can absorb, and the many great ways you can apply it to make your life better and better.

Affirmation:

I eagerly keep learning and growing more each day.

Day 191

You must lose a fly to catch a trout.

– George Herbert

George Herbert's wise words are a great reminder about the benefits of sacrifice when pursuing our goals and dreams. Most often the things we have to sacrifice are our time and energy. Some people feel annoyed about having to visualize or meditate repeatedly; they begrudge the repetitive effort necessary to transform their thoughts from negative to positive, and they otherwise resist the transition from who they were to who they want to become.

Have you ever felt annoyed by the sacrifices you've had to make in your own life? If so, it may be helpful to focus more on the many benefits you stand to gain rather than focusing keenly on what you're "losing" when you sacrifice. Rather than feeling annoyed about the time and effort required to improve your life, do your best to see it as a welcome exercise in self-discipline and keep affirming that your sacrifices will yield great rewards in the long run.

Affirmation:

I am always gaining much more than I'm losing.

Day 192

Waste no tears over the grieves of yesterday.

– Euripides

Have you ever looked back upon the events of the day and realized that your focus was terrible? Perhaps you started the day with great intentions to stay focused on abundance and joy, but then experienced obstacles, setbacks and challenges repeatedly until finally you gave up trying to stay positive – and the rest of your day just spiraled further down into negativity. At the end of the day when you realize that you didn't stick to your intention, you may be tempted to feel upset with yourself, but that would be the worst thing you can do.

A better option is to mentally relive the day and change anything you don't like. For example, if you got upset about financial turmoil, go back to those moments in your mind and choose the reaction you would have liked to have instead. You won't change the events that have already passed – but you will feel more empowered about them. As you feel more empowered you will begin attracting better outcomes from this moment on.

Affirmation:

I can rewrite the script of my life at any time.

Day 193

From small beginnings come great things.

– Proverb

One of the easiest ways to begin making positive changes in your life is to scale back your efforts so they feel more manageable. Most people take the opposite approach and try to conquer every negative thought and habit in one fell swoop. However, as the above proverb states, great things can indeed come from small beginnings. A small beginning can be a subtle shift in your dominant thoughts, or a slight change in the actions you take every day.

The important thing is to listen to your intuition about what feels right for you. While one person may feel comfortable taking on greater challenges, you may feel overwhelmed by it. For every aspect of your life that you wish to change, think about smaller improvements you can begin right now. It might be a soothing affirmation that all is well, or reducing the time you spend with negative people. No matter how small or subtle these changes may seem at first glance, they can be powerful enough to bring about great things in your life.

Affirmation:

I can handle small changes confidently.

Day 194

If there is no struggle, there is no progress.

– Frederick Douglass

Most of us have been taught that progress comes from struggle, but when it comes to the Law of Attraction struggle is one sure way to block our progress. This is not because of the physical aspects of the struggle, but rather the emotional essence of the struggle that simply draws more of what we are focusing upon. When we are locked in struggle, what feelings do we transmit to the universe? Despair, frustration, aggravation – and all of these feelings will continue to attract more situations in which we will feel like that.

On the other hand, when we get our thoughts and feelings aligned with joy and ease (no matter which goal we are working toward), we immediately begin "asking" the universe to keep sending more and more situations where we feel joyful and relaxed. As a result, we experience fewer problems and challenges as we work toward our goals – and in fact, in every aspect of our lives as well.

Affirmation:

In my world, progress comes from joy and ease.

Day 195

What we see depends mainly on what we look for.

- John Lubbock

It's easy to forget how much power your expectations have, especially when it comes to using the Law of Attraction. Have you ever accidentally "expected" a negative outcome and created it in your life? For example, perhaps you had to take your vehicle to the auto shop for repairs and you worried that the bill would be expensive, and it was. What might have happened if you had deliberately expected a better outcome instead?

Negative expectations have become a way of life for many of us, but they do not have to be our reality if we get into the habit of choosing something better. If you would like to turn this habit around in your own life, start today by deliberately choosing better expectations. When you feel worried or uncertain about something, deliberately choose a positive outcome and then put your full focus on expecting it to happen. Then watch in awe as the universe begins treating those positive expectations as "requests" and answers many (if not most) of them from now on.

Affirmation:

I expect the best, always!

Day 196

Ideas are like rabbits. You get a couple and learn how to handle them, and pretty soon you have a dozen.

- John Steinbeck

Inspired guidance can seem fleeting when you first begin working with the Law of Attraction to create an abundant life. At first it may seem like your mind goes blank when you try to come up with ideas for increasing your income or setting bigger goals. However, as John Steinbeck so humorously demonstrates above, ideas (especially inspired ideas from the universe) have a way of multiplying quickly once you open that creative flow.

A good way to avoid creativity overload is to start keeping an idea journal. Make it a regular habit to spend time sitting quietly each day, allowing creative ideas to come to you and jotting each one down in your journal. You may not put all of them into action, and you don't have to. Simply writing them down and acknowledging them as possibilities is often enough to keep the creative stream of inspiration flowing.

Affirmation:

I am open to an endless stream of creative ideas.

Day 197

Self-pity gets you nowhere. One must have the adventurous daring to accept oneself as a bundle of possibilities and undertake the most interesting game in the world -- making the most of one's best.

- Harry Emerson Fosdick

Have you ever gotten stuck in feelings of self-pity? Most of us have at one time or another – but some of us have made a regular habit of it. If this is a trend that keeps repeating in your life it's important to take it seriously because what you are doing is telling the universe that you are "a victim" – and the universe will simply keep sending more and more situations that make you feel victimized and powerless.

As Harry Emerson Fosdick suggests above, if you instead begin to see yourself as a "bundle of possibilities" and remember that you always have options to improve your circumstances, you will quickly realize that there is no reason to feel sorry for yourself. Even if not everything in your life is perfect or wonderful, you will still know that you can begin choosing better thoughts, feelings and actions that will change your life for the better – no self-pity required.

Affirmation:

I always have the option to choose something better.

Day 198

Not only is there a right to be happy, there is a duty to be happy. So much sadness exists in the world that we are all under obligation to contribute as much joy as lies within our powers.

- John S. Bonnell

One of the most important reasons to create a more abundant life for yourself is that you will be better able to help others too. You can certainly help others even if you don't have a lot of money, time or resources, but obviously your ability to help more people more often increases if you have greater abundance. However, before any of this can happen you must believe, as John Bonnell so eloquently states above, that you have a duty to be happy and abundant.

If you don't believe that being happy and abundant is your duty (or even your right), you can't place yourself in a position to help others improve their lives either. Starting today, make it your most important goal to build a rock-solid belief that you deserve to be as successful, abundant and happy as you can be. Once you truly believe it, begin demonstrating to others that they also have the same duty in their own lives and you will be giving them the greatest gift they will ever receive.

Affirmation:

It is my duty to be as happy and abundant as possible.

Day 199

When in doubt, make a fool of yourself. There is a microscopically thin line between being brilliantly creative and acting like the most gigantic idiot on earth. So, what the hell, leap.

- Cynthia Heimel

Cynthia Heimel offers a refreshing, carefree perspective on risk – one that most of us would do well to apply in our own lives. Have you ever held back on doing something because you were afraid you might make a mistake and look "stupid"? Or perhaps you worried that you might fail or that other people would think badly of you. If so, you can probably recall the intense feelings of tension and unease that resulted from such limited thinking.

As Ms. Heimel reminds us, there is a very fine line between creative brilliance and foolishness – but creative brilliance cannot emerge unless you take the actions that allow it expression. There is always a risk of feeling foolish if it doesn't work out the way you planned, but when you consider that the only alternative is to not try at all and therefore never make any progress, the risk suddenly seems inconsequential.

Affirmation:

Expressing my creative brilliance is worth the risk of feeling foolish.

Day 200

You know you are on the road to success if you would do your job, and not be paid for it.

– Oprah Winfrey

Oprah Winfrey is undoubtedly one of the most successful women in the world, and her statement above reveals a key reason why she has been able to achieve so much in her career – she loves what she does so much that she would want to do it even if she wasn't being paid. How many people in the world can truly say that about their work? More importantly, can you say that about your work?

If not, it may be time to consider whether the career path you are currently walking is the right one to lead you to the success you desire. Even if you know it isn't, that doesn't mean you have to make drastic career changes immediately. You don't have to quit your job because it's not your deepest passion in life, but you may want to spend some time thinking about the kind of work you would truly love to do; the kind of work that you would gladly do without pay – and consider some ways to begin moving toward that work, even if you do it gradually.

Affirmation:

I awaken my greatest passion now.

Day 201

It's easy to have faith in yourself and have discipline when you're a winner, when you're number one. What you got to have is faith and discipline when you're not a winner

- Vince Lombardi

Attracting abundance is very much like achieving any goal; you have to exert a lot of effort, have a lot of patience, and firmly believe that someday soon your results will come. This is often one of the most challenging parts of deliberate creation for many people because they don't yet have "proof" that the Law of Attraction works. The lack of evidence makes them feel like maybe they shouldn't get too immersed in the process in case it doesn't work out.

Unfortunately, belief is a major ingredient in successfully attracting the things you want. The stronger and more consistent your belief is, the faster and more consistent your results will usually be. So, how can you build a rock-solid belief when you haven't yet seen much "proof" that your efforts will pay off? One good way is to insist, over and over again, that you intend to make progress. The moment you start to see glimmers of progress in your own life your intensity of belief will skyrocket, which makes future manifestations much easier.

Affirmation:

As I look for evidence of progress, it appears.

Day 202

The worst wheel of the cart makes the most noise.

- Benjamin Franklin

When it comes to drawing more wealth into your life, it's worthwhile to take a close look at your behaviors day to day and see if your speech habits might be hindering your progress. One common thing that many people do without realizing it is complain continuously about some facet of the very thing they are trying to attract into their lives. For example, complaining about how selfish rich people are, or how "the little guy" never gets a break.

These types of complaints may seem harmless, but they have the power to unbalance your entire "cart" of abundance, just as a damaged or loose wheel would. You cannot love and hate something at the same time. You can't desire it and resent it at the same time. To attract abundance you have to adore abundance – in ALL of its forms – including the fact that other people may have more of it than you do at the moment. Feel glad for them, and you direct that same energy of love and appreciation toward yourself too.

Affirmation:

I appreciate every expression of abundance, even in other people.

Day 203

*Youth is a circumstance you can't do anything about.
The trick is to grow up without getting old.*

- Frank Lloyd Wright

Do you ever feel like attracting greater abundance is
taking way too long? Like you are simply spinning
your wheels and getting nowhere? In some ways this
is similar to a child who can't wait to grow up and
begin living his or her own life – and in what seems
like a blink of the eye, forty or fifty years flies by and
they find themselves longing for the innocence and
enthusiasm of their youth. They may have spent
decades of their life always looking forward to a better
future, and in doing so missed out on the joys of the
present moment.

This same concept applies to your intention to attract
abundance into your life. If you spend all of your time
wishing you could leap ahead into a more abundant
future, you are missing a phenomenal opportunity to
appreciate the abundance you already have. The
irony here is that the more you recognize and
appreciate the abundance you have right here and
now, the more energy and intention you are investing
into that lavish, abundant future you long for – and
you'll achieve it without sacrificing your happiness
now.

Affirmation:

I create my future with what I focus on here and now.

Day 204

Trust the instinct to the end, though you can render no reason.

- Ralph Waldo Emerson

You can study the art of manifesting abundance for decades and still not quite "get it" until you put it into action and work with the principles each day. The more you practice directing your thoughts, choosing more positive emotional states and building your belief, the stronger your ability will become. Even more importantly, you will begin to develop an "instinct" about the right thoughts and actions to attract anything you want.

Some people may think of this instinct as "intuition" or "divine guidance" – but the name you apply to it isn't as important as recognizing that it exists and is available to you at all times. If you haven't yet become aware of this instinct within yourself, you can begin working with it by asking the universe for guidance each day. Think about your goals and ask for insights and ideas that will help you to achieve them more easily. Then be on the lookout for guidance that may come as creative ideas, people, "hunches" or other synchronicities that provide opportunities.

Affirmation:

I keep my mind and heart open to receive guidance.

Day 205

Quality means doing it right when no one is looking.

- Henry Ford

Do you ever feel like you are simply "going through the motions" as you attempt to attract more money into your life? Do you perform visualizations or recite affirmations halfheartedly and put little effort into them, even though you sincerely want to receive more abundance? Do you ever procrastinate and avoid working on your goals, then get angry with yourself for your "laziness"? There can be many reasons for a lack of quality effort like this, and most have nothing to do with laziness.

More often, there is a hidden agenda taking place beneath the surface. Perhaps you feel uncertain that your efforts will pay off so you hesitate to spend too much time and energy on the activities. Or maybe some part of you feels uncomfortable about the idea of having more money, so you subconsciously resist taking the steps that will attract abundance. A good way to find out for sure is to make a list of all the "negative" things you can think of that may happen as a result of having more abundance. Every item on that list is a clue as to why you may be resisting it.

Affirmation:

I am releasing all resistance to abundance starting now.

Day 206

Build up your weaknesses until they become your strong points.

- Knute Rockne

The process of attracting what you want is much like any other skill; there are several steps that need to be mastered before success can be realized. Most people will find that they are naturally good at some parts of the attraction process, and not so good at others. It can be worthwhile to set aside some time to identify your own areas of strength and weakness, and then do your best to build up the weak areas until they become strengths.

The main aspects of the attraction process are: getting clear about what you want, believing you can have it, knowing it is already on the way, letting go and trusting that the universe will deliver it, and staying alert for possible inspired actions that may help bring the end result into being. Think carefully about each of these steps and consider whether you frequently falter with any of them. If so, do what you can to strengthen your skills in that area and see what a difference it can make in your results.

Affirmation:

I am mastering each step in the attraction process.

Day 207

Forgiveness is the fragrance that the violet sheds on the heel that has crushed it.

- Mark Twain

Since beginning your conscious creation journey, have you had days where you felt like you just couldn't get it right? Days where your concentration was off, or your emotions seemed to swing wildly no matter how hard you tried to keep them in check? It's a natural occurrence for most of us even after we have gained some level of proficiency with the Law of Attraction, and the temptation to get upset about it is strong.

One of the best ways to ease the intensity of days like this is to practice the art of forgiveness. When you notice that you're starting to feel angry or impatient with yourself, say something like this: "I'm not sure why I feel so scattered and negative today, but I forgive myself for being human. I forgive the negative thoughts that keep popping into my head, and I forgive myself for getting emotional about them. It's okay to have an off day now and then; but I'm doing pretty well considering, and I'm proud of myself for that."

Affirmation:

I forgive myself and move forward a little wiser.

Day 208

If you are not willing to risk the unusual, you will have to settle for the ordinary.

- Jim Rohn

One of the great things about the Law of Attraction is that knowledge and mastery of it allows us to transcend the limitations that are often placed upon us by other people and ourselves. Awakening to our power as deliberate creators suddenly makes all of our dreams and goals seem possible. Everything we have ever wanted is now within our reach, and we can't wait to get started attracting them right away!

However, in order to achieve our lofty goals and dreams, we may have to make a few sacrifices along the way. We'll have to step out of our comfort zones to take action, even if we initially feel nervous about it. We'll have to develop a belief that we deserve to have more abundance; and we'll have to be willing to let go of situations and relationships that no longer serve our highest good. These changes become a bit easier to make if we can remember that we are in the process of releasing an "ordinary" lifestyle in favor of one that is extraordinary.

Affirmation:

I deserve an extraordinary life.

Day 209

An early-morning walk is a blessing for the whole day.

- Henry David Thoreau

Henry David Thoreau's words above share a great insight about the power of immersing yourself in peacefulness, beauty and reconnection to your inner spirit first thing in the morning. Whether you choose to achieve this balanced state by taking a walk, writing in a gratitude journal, or visualizing something inspiring – you will be setting the tone for the whole day if you do these activities before the busyness of the day takes over.

Take a moment right now and consider what most of your mornings are usually like. Do you jump out of bed and immediately launch into physical action? If so, you may want to adjust your routine to allow a few minutes of quiet reflection first. You may feel that you can't spare the time, but once you realize the power of this activity you will quickly find a way to make it a priority, even if it means rearranging a few things in your schedule, or waking up a few minutes earlier than you usually would.

Affirmation:

I give myself permission to reflect and reconnect each morning.

Day 210

Take time to deliberate; but when the time for action arrives, stop thinking and go in.

- Andrew Jackson

Have you ever felt a nudge to take a specific action but felt unsure about whether you should do it or not? "Inspired action" is one concept that many deliberate creators have a difficult time grasping. How can you tell for sure if you're being given an inspired action or if it's just wishful thinking? What if you take the action and nothing happens? What if you take it and something bad happens? Fears and uncertainties like these can often lead to confusion and paralysis.

The majority of inspired actions will usually have three things in common: they will seem fun or exciting; they will be relatively easy to accomplish; and they will not have serious repercussions attached to them. Also keep in mind that you are never required to take a specific action, even if the universe is nudging you to do so. You do have the right to hold back if you don't feel ready to move forward, but with most inspired actions you'll feel eager to take them.

Affirmation:

If I feel inspired by the idea, it's probably an inspired action.

Day 211

Great minds have purposes, others have wishes.

- Washington Irving

One of the determining factors in making your dreams a reality is the strength of your intention to do so. Most of the manifestation techniques you may be familiar with are fairly passive in nature – such as visualizing, reciting affirmations, creating vision boards, and keeping a gratitude journal. These activities are powerful because they help keep your thoughts focused on what you want, rather than things you don't want – but alone they can only take you so far.

A much more "active" technique is honing the intensity of your intentions and belief. It's one thing to visualize something you want, but can you feel the power in also intending to have it and fiercely believing it will be yours? Intention and belief represent the line that is drawn between wishes and purposes. Don't just "wish" for your dreams to be reality – intend that they will be; believe it with all of your might and you will contribute much stronger energy to making it happen.

Affirmation:

I intend and know that my abundant reality is on its way!

Day 212

The only thing we know about the future is that it will be different.

- Peter F. Drucker

As you get more and more proficient with using the Law of Attraction, you begin to realize that every day of your life literally begins as a blank canvas that you can paint any way you like. You can choose the amount of money you want to have in the bank, the income you want to earn, and the quality of lifestyle you wish to live. By the power of your thoughts, intentions, beliefs and actions, you can determine all of this and more.

When you really "get this" and begin seeing the evidence of your thoughts creating your reality, you will find that you won't be able to go back to being an "unconscious creator". You won't be able to blame other people and circumstances for your problems and difficulties. While this may be unsettling to some people, truly embracing this knowledge gives you much more power to keep improving your life because you will know without a doubt that any and all challenges can be overcome with a simple shift in mind-set. And that is true empowerment.

Affirmation:

I paint the canvas of my life according to what I focus on.

Day 213

Did you ever see an unhappy horse? Did you ever see a bird that had the blues? One reason why birds and horses are not unhappy is because they are not trying to impress other birds and horses.

- Dale Carnegie

Dale Carnegie's insight above is a powerful one that can easily be applied to your intention to attract abundance. Have you ever considered why you want to be more abundant? What are your underlying motivations? When you think about having plenty of abundance, what are some of the images that pop into your mind? Do you envision having a large home, taking trips around the world, driving the latest and greatest sports car? Or do you crave a quieter, less stressful lifestyle not too far removed from the one you are living right now?

It's important to examine your desires in this way because wanting the right things for the wrong reasons can create dissatisfying outcomes. If you are driven by the need to feel important or impress people with your success, you are basing your happiness on a faulty foundation that will not support lasting result. A better approach would be to focus on manifesting the lifestyle that makes you feel inspired, joyful and free – regardless of what others may think about you.

Affirmation:

I am getting clearer on what I want and why I want it.

Day 214

Self-confidence is the first requisite to great undertakings.

- Samuel Johnson

Confidence is a vital part of learning to use the Law of Attraction effectively. The first place to begin building up your confidence is within yourself; having confidence in your own abilities as a deliberate creator. The first few manifestations you attempt may not work immediately, or at all. However, as you keep strengthening your belief and working with the techniques, you begin to see results and your confidence continues growing from there.

Equally important is building your confidence in a loving, supportive universe. One of the best and simplest ways to start is by opening the lines of communication between yourself and the universe. Start by spending 5 to 10 minutes each morning communicating your desires and asking for guidance. Then sit quietly for a few more minutes, staying open to any insights you receive. Before long you will notice that guidance comes along when you need it most, building your confidence and dramatically enhancing your results.

Affirmation:

I believe in myself, and I believe in a supportive universe.

Day 215

You've got to say, "I think that if I keep working at this and want it badly enough I can have it." It's called perseverance.

- Lee Iacocca

Sometimes when you attempt to manifest something, it seems like nothing goes right. You may spend days or weeks visualizing and using all of the "tricks and tools" you have at your disposal, but you see no progress at all – or situations and events seem to get worse instead of better. Has this ever happened to you? If so, you may have been tempted to believe that the universe was telling you that your desire will not be granted, but that may not necessarily be so.

More often than not, the culprit is one or more limiting beliefs. You may have inner blockages, resistance or fear that is not allowing your desire to manifest. To break through these obstacles, tell the universe firmly that you are not giving up; ask to be shown why your manifestation attempts have not been working so far, and what you might do to change this. Then keep on the lookout over the next few days and you will likely be led to a clue or two that help you dissolve the blockages and begin making progress more easily.

Affirmation:

All blockages fade in the light of clarity.

Day 216

Laziness may appear attractive, but work gives satisfaction.

- Anne Frank

One of the things that appealed to many of us regarding the Law of Attraction is that it was "easier" than creating purely through physical effort. As we began to work with the principles, however, we quickly learned that even if less physical effort was required we still had to expend a fair amount of mental and emotional effort in order to attract the things we wanted. Sometimes that effort can seem like a chore – especially when we're not yet seeing much progress.

Anne Frank offers a great insight to help make our efforts seem less draining; feel satisfied by the work itself. Have you ever felt proud of yourself for a job well done? Have you enjoyed a sense of elation when a long, challenging task was finally completed? Apply this same concept to your manifestation efforts. Tell yourself that you'll feel proud and satisfied when you've finished doing the work – then push yourself to do it even if you don't feel like it initially, and bask in the feelings of accomplishment you'll enjoy afterward.

Affirmation:

I am proud of myself for giving my best effort.

Day 217

Regret for wasted time is more wasted time.

- Mason Cooley

A common mistake made by many Law of Attraction practitioners is trying to figure out where they may have gone wrong. They spend days or weeks working to improve their thoughts, they start feeling better, circumstances in their lives start to improve – and then they'll experience a financial upheaval (or several) that shakes their confidence and makes them wonder, "How did this happen? What did I do wrong?" Then they start reviewing their thoughts and actions over the past few weeks, trying to find the error so they can "fix" it.

Have you ever done this? Unfortunately this only makes things worse because actively "looking" for errors will only keep creating more of them. A more productive response would be to say to yourself, "Okay, this upheaval is happening and I'm not sure why, but my job is to focus on what I want to experience. How would I like this situation to turn out?" Once you know the answer to that question, focus on it with all of your power and you should clear any negative influences that may have contributed to the upheaval in the first place.

Affirmation:

Regardless of challenges, I choose to direct my thoughts positively now

Day 218

Of course there is no formula for success except perhaps an unconditional acceptance of life and what it brings.

- Arthur Rubinstein

There is immense power in living your life from a calm, detached state of mind. Where the Law of Attraction is concerned, being "attached" to specific events and conditions can cause problems because your very attachment communicates a message of fear and lack to the universe. The more you feel as if you "need" to have something, the more you will reinforce your reality of not having it – and the universe will keep sending more of that reality to you.

On the other hand, if you do as Mr. Rubinstein recommends above and adopt a relaxed, unconditional acceptance of life and all that it brings to you, you communicate a very different message to the universe. In all areas of your life you will be affirming, "All is well; I feel good; I can handle this . . ." and the universe must return more situations that will make you feel that way. Even better, this mind-set instantly makes you more receptive to the specific outcomes you have been eager to receive but couldn't while you were grasping at them.

Affirmation:

I choose to remain detached and calm in every situation.

Day 219

The essence of all beautiful art, all great art, is gratitude.

- Friedrich Nietzsche

A lot has been written about the power of gratitude over the years, and it's an excellent way to begin shifting your thoughts and attracting more abundance into your life. But you may not have considered that gratitude is more than a feeling – it is an "essence" of energy that you can pour into everything you do each day – and as you radiate the essence of gratitude (which is really the essence of abundance), you will immediately begin attracting more of the same back to you.

What if you were to infuse your financial challenges with the essence of gratitude? What if you could embrace them rather than resist them – and be truly thankful for the clarity and strength they inspire within you? When you focus on the positive side of a situation, you cannot help but expand that quality in your life. The challenging aspects of the situation may not dissolve instantly, but you won't mind because you will be too busy feeling grateful for the lessons they impart to you.

Affirmation:

I am a bottomless well of gratitude.

Day 220

There are three constants in life . . . change, choice and principles.

- Stephen R. Covey

Not many of us appreciate change – especially when it relates to our level of abundance – because change is often messy and frightening. However, having an awareness of the Law of Attraction gives us a certain measure of control over change because, as Stephen Covey points out, we do always have choices. When a challenge or obstacle appears in our path, our greatest power lies in that moment because our reaction to it determines what happens next.

Getting upset and feeling powerless about the situation only strengthens it, while pausing to affirm our power and make a conscious choice about the outcome we want to experience is often enough to have a positive effect. When it comes right down to it, we cannot avoid change, nor would we want to. Change prevents stagnation and boredom. It provides opportunities to keep growing and evolving, and it is always positive as long as we use the power of our intentions to make the most of the changes that come our way.

Affirmation:

I eagerly embrace change in my life.

Day 221

It is always with excitement that I wake up in the morning wondering what my intuition will toss up to me, like gifts from the sea. I work with it and rely on it. It's my partner.

- Jonas Salk

When it comes to attracting more abundance into your life, it's hard to deny the power that lies in allowing your intuition to guide you. However, Jonas Salk implies something important with his statement above – and that is expecting to receive the guidance you desire. Many people only scratch the surface of what is possible by failing to build confidence and conviction in their own intuitive insights, and therefore never learn to truly trust and rely on it.

Just like muscles, your intuition must be exercised regularly to become strong. Likewise, you also have to exercise your own receptivity and awareness to better understand the messages and insights your intuition provides. As Mr. Salk suggests, work with your intuition regularly and come to rely on it as a partner in attracting abundance. Over time your confidence will grow and you will come to expect and believe in the guidance, which will inspire more of it to come.

Affirmation:

My intuition is always leading me to greater abundance.

Day 222

Kites rise highest against the wind - not with it.

- Winston Churchill

One of the biggest reasons why people try to attract greater abundance is because they are tired of financial challenges. It's true that having limited financial resources can make many aspects of life more difficult – but have you ever considered that your financial challenges have provided a valuable benefit by helping you to better clarify the type of life you would rather be living? Without challenges, blessings would not seem so inspiring by comparison.

"The wind" that Winston Churchill refers to above could be represented in your own life as your challenges, fears, limiting beliefs and struggles. As much as you would probably love to wave a magic wand and banish them forever, doing so would not serve you because there would be nothing to inspire you to greater heights and ever-increasing levels of abundance. Like a kite, you need the wind in order to soar.

Affirmation:

My challenges only inspire me to soar higher.

Day 223

I will study and get ready, and perhaps my chance will come.

- Abraham Lincoln

Abraham Lincoln shares a glimpse of a powerful habit that you can apply with great success in your own life, and that is the act of preparation. Most of us are taught not to get our hopes up, not to do things to "jinx" ourselves and our chances for success by assuming too much and taking action before the time is right. However, the opposite approach should be taken when it comes to the Law of Attraction.

How much have you done to prepare for the arrival of your abundance? Have you created room for it? Have you thought about the changes it will create in your life and prepared accordingly to handle them? If not, you may want to begin doing that today. Grab a notebook and make a list of the changes you believe would result from having more abundance, and then explore ways to prepare yourself for them – both mentally and physically.

Affirmation:

I am prepared to receive my abundance now.

Day 224

Avoiding the phrase "I don't have time..." will soon help you to realize that you do have the time needed for just about anything you choose to accomplish in life.

- Bo Bennett

One of the more powerful uses for the Law of Attraction is ensuring that you always have time to work on attracting more abundance into your life. Have you ever felt that you were too rushed to spend time meditating, visualizing, creating vision boards, and so on? What you may not realize is that being short on time is yet another expression of lack that can be turned around with right thinking. Try the following exercise and watch how it miraculously seems to stretch time.

Each morning when you awaken, spend five minutes sitting quietly, breathing deeply and affirming that you always have more than enough time to do everything you need to do. During the rest of the day if you begin to feel rushed or harried, pause and once again affirm that you always have plenty of time – and then deliberately slow down your pace. Before long you'll notice that time does indeed seem to slow down and your somehow able to complete everything, including things you really want to do – with time to spare.

Affirmation:

Time is nothing more than a perception that I can change.

Day 225

Optimism means expecting the best, but confidence means knowing how to handle the worst. Never make a move if you are merely optimistic.

- The Zurich Axioms

Optimism and confidence are important qualities to have if you want to improve your financial well-being, and they should work in harmony for best results. Many people are optimistic that they can someday improve their lives, but they don't always feel confident in their ability to do so. Worse, in the face of repetitive obstacles and challenges they may even lose their sense of optimism and slip back into a disempowered state of mind.

To prevent this from happening to you, make it a habit to actively exercise your optimism and confidence daily. Start the day by affirming that great abundance, resources, opportunities and people will come to you. Don't just "hope" for it – be absolutely convinced that it's going to happen. Then, if you encounter a situation that unsettles you, gather your courage and insist with unshakable confidence that despite appearances, all is well. The more you do this, the more you will come to believe it, and the more you believe it the more it will become your reality.

Affirmation:

I am optimistic and confident, always.

Day 226

Take the attitude of a student. Never be too big to ask questions. Never know too much to learn something new.

- Og Mandino

Og Mandino's excellent suggestion is a great way to really harness the power of the creation process in your life, whether it pertains to abundance or any other subject. Too often we feel that we've seen and done it all and there is nothing left to learn – but that can be a dangerous attitude that only stunts our growth. The following exercise will help you to keep expanding your knowledge and passion for the Law of Attraction, and finding ways to apply it with great results.

Each night before you go to sleep, write down one lesson you learned during the day. The lesson can be something empowering, inspiring, amazing, or even humbling – but it should be something that you can apply to other situations in your life from this moment on. Jot down a few ideas for applying the insight in the future, and then spend a few minutes feeling grateful for the insight and the situation that caused the insight to appear.

Affirmation:

I learn something fascinating every day.

Day 227

Don't find fault, find a remedy.

- Henry Ford

Henry Ford's blunt advice is a perfect fit for the intention to manifest more abundance in your life.

You may be like most other people in the sense that when something negative happens, you tend to focus upon it obsessively, complain about it, find endless reasons why you aren't happy with the way things are, and so on. From a manifestation standpoint this creates a big problem because you will keep infusing more and more energy into the very situation you don't want to keep experiencing.

As Henry Ford suggests, focusing on finding a remedy is much more effective, and using the Law of Attraction to do this is amazingly easy: simply turn your focus toward the solution you would like to experience. What kind of outcome do you want to experience in this situation? Keep focusing on that outcome exclusively, and sooner than you expect it circumstances will begin to shift in a more positive direction.

Affirmation:

All problems – and their solutions – are born from my own consciousness.

Day 228

*In order for the light to shine so brightly, the
darkness must be present.*

- Francis Bacon

Today's quote provides a great reminder that the
sum total of our lives are a delicate balance
between good and bad, positive and negative. As
much as you may think that you would be happier if
the negative stuff didn't exist, you would also have
no point of reference for the better experiences you
are striving to create. In fact, recognizing your
challenges and problems as opportunities to
exercise your creative focus makes them instantly
become more bearable.

Rather than fighting against the things that bother
you, simply use them as a starting point to choose
something better. For example, if you constantly
struggle financially, figure out how much money or
income you would prefer to have and intend to be
shown a way to achieve that objective. Every time
you are faced with another experience of financial
difficulty, reassert your intention to allow more
money into your life. The more you keep focusing
on the outcome you want, the faster you will tip the
balance from lack to abundance.

Affirmation:

I am grateful for challenges because they motivate
me to choose something better.

Day 229

Nearly all men can stand adversity, but if you want to test a man's character, give him power.

- Abraham Lincoln

This great quote by Abraham Lincoln offers an insightful angle on the challenges you may face as a deliberate creator. When you first begin trying to attract greater abundance you may have visions of a lifestyle that is easier, more peaceful and more enjoyable. However, when you really start to think about receiving and handling large sums of money, you may feel uncomfortable about the inevitable changes that would come along with having more money.

Not only can these changes test your character, they can test your confidence, peace of mind, and happiness in ways that you may not yet be prepared to handle. As a result, you may subconsciously block abundance from entering your life. One good way to overcome these uncertainties is to focus on gradually building up your level of abundance instead of trying to make huge leaps all at once. Then you give yourself time to adjust to the changes and ease into greater abundance.

Affirmation:

I gradually attract greater abundance and develop the confidence to handle it easily.

Day 230

When what we are is what we want to be, that's happiness.

- Malcolm S. Forbes

Malcolm Forbes's insight can be taken in multiple contexts, one of which would be the power of "being" what you are trying to create with the Law of Attraction. For example, visualizing an abundant life experience for your future is a good way to start the creative process, but even more effective is practicing the feeling of having great abundance in your life right now. The greatest benefit to doing this is that it creates cohesion between your present reality and the reality you want to be living in the future.

The best way to practice being abundant right now is to "pretend" several times throughout the day. As you shop in stores, for example, pause for a moment and imagine what it would feel like to know that you could easily purchase anything you wanted. As you dine out, imagine being able to order from the menu without even glancing at the prices. As you lay down to sleep at night, imagine what it would be like to have total financial peace of mind. The more you think about these things, the more you will be adopting the energetic frequency of great abundance.

Affirmation:

I am steadily becoming the abundant person I want to be.

Day 231

In every difficult situation is potential value. Believe this, then begin looking for it.

- Norman Vincent Peale

When you consider difficult financial situations, there may not seem to be any value in them at first glance. However, there is a strong clue in Dr. Peale's quote above, and that is, "begin looking for it". The more you expect to see something you will come into alignment with it and start noticing more of it. This is true even in the most difficult circumstances; if you begin actively looking for something good about the situation; an opportunity, a solution, a gift of some kind, those good qualities and opportunities can become actualized.

Try this experiment right now: List a few of your more difficult life experiences and then come up with one thing that you are grateful for regarding each situation. It may be something you learned from the experience, or an unexpected blessing that arose from it, or anything positive. Writing it down and acknowledging the positive aspects of it can help you to keep recognizing even more positive qualities, even in the midst of your current challenges.

Affirmation:

I can find something to be grateful for in every situation.

Day 232

It is easier to prevent bad habits than to break them.

- Benjamin Franklin

Benjamin Franklin's words apply beautifully to your abundance-attraction endeavors because as you have probably already discovered, changing negative thought habits regarding money can seem monumentally difficult at times. This is especially true when chronic thoughts have manifested into full blown financial difficulties. The harder you try to think more positively about abundance, the more conditions around you seem to challenge that intention.

The good news is that with every passing minute that you work on improving your thoughts, you are creating a solid positive thought habit that will eventually override the old, negative thoughts. Then, as long as you keep actively reinforcing your positive thinking habit, the more you will be preventing negative thoughts from taking over your mind and manifesting into corresponding outcomes in your life.

Affirmation:

Through the power of repetition I am creating a rock-solid abundance consciousness.

Day 233

Happiness is when what you think, what you say, and what you do are in harmony.

- Mahatma Gandhi

As you start visualizing greater abundance, you are communicating a strong energetic signal that the universe begins to respond to by sending more abundance your way. However, every time you then notice that your abundance hasn't yet arrived, or you get emotionally distraught by financial problems, you are emitting a conflicting energetic signal that says, "I don't have enough money, I feel frustrated by financial problems," and so on.

Unfortunately, the universe also begins responding to this signal, so you end up receiving mixed results from the two conflicting signals. To create harmony in your signal, you have to find a way to stop communicating a negative signal and keep your signal as positive as possible. You can do this by visualizing, saying positive affirmations, and most importantly, holding positive expectations even when your circumstances don't seem very optimistic at the moment.

Affirmation:

I am always conscious of the signal I am communicating to the universe.

Day 234

There is nothing like a dream to create the future.

- Victor Hugo

Have you ever felt disillusioned about visualizing and intending a more abundant life experience? Sometimes this happens because you have gathered a lifetime of disappointment as you tried in vain to improve chronic problems, including financial problems. Unfortunately, continuous disappointments like this can push you into a state of resignation about the way things are, which leaves little motivation for making positive changes.

A good way to overcome a state of resignation is to recognize the true power of your thoughts in turning your life around, even if you don't yet have any ideas about how to do so. As Victor Hugo suggests, dreaming is what starts the creative process, so it follows that you can get things moving in a positive direction simply by daring to dream about something wonderful that you would like to experience. Don't worry about how it will be realized – just imagine how wonderful it would feel to experience it and allow the rest to flow into place naturally.

Affirmation:

I give myself permission to dream of an abundant, joyful future.

Day 235

I never did anything by accident, nor did any of my inventions come by accident; they came by work.

- Thomas Edison

Thomas Edison's quote above holds a gem of wisdom that can be easily applied to your attempts to attract more abundance – but you may want to replace the word "work" with "dedication". Work isn't a bad thing, nor should its merits be discounted completely, but the word itself gives the impression that all success is a result of physical action alone. Deliberate creators know that attitude is equally as important as action steps to achieve a certain outcome.

Dedication is a better word choice because it is necessary in both mental and physical contexts. The more dedicated you are about creating an abundant lifestyle, the more diligently you will apply your effort to improving your thoughts, dissolving limiting beliefs, and taking inspired action on a daily basis. Rather than expecting immediate results, you'll develop the confidence to move steadily and consistently toward the outcomes you want – and none of your success will seem accidental.

Affirmation:

I am dedicated to consistent effort, both mentally and physically.

Day 236

Let us always meet each other with smile, for the smile is the beginning of love.

- Mother Teresa

Mother Teresa's words share the important message about treating other people with love and kindness, but did you know that you can also use this concept to attract more abundance into your life? How often do you awaken in the morning with a smile and a feeling of gratitude for the many expressions of abundance all around you? How often do you think about your blessings and affirm that many more like them will soon begin flooding into your life?

If you don't do these things often, you may want to start as soon as possible because they have the power to immediately shift you into an empowered state of mind and emotion. And the more empowered you feel about abundance, the more easily you can begin attracting more of it into your life. If you struggle to move into a true state of gratitude and love at first, try simply repeating, "Thank you for this moment" over and over several times a day. Eventually you should feel an inner shift taking place so that genuine feelings of gratitude become easier.

Affirmation:

I flow feelings of gratitude and love toward all forms of abundance.

Day 237

Weakness of attitude becomes weakness of character.

– Albert Einstein

It may seem strange to think about your attitude being "weak" but when you consider the power of thoughts it makes perfect sense. The less you work at focusing your thoughts deliberately, the more they will randomly jump around on many different topics, including abundance. The problem with this is that you will not be consistently focusing on the outcome you want, so you will not be able to direct your energy toward it, and nothing much will change.

In that case, we might reword Albert Einstein's quote to read, "Weakness of attitude becomes weakness of reality". To develop strength of attitude, all you need to do is consistently work your mindset, just like you would work your physical muscles during an exercise routine. Deliberately and consistently think positively about money and all forms of abundance as often as you can. This will quickly strengthen your attitude and start attracting a reality to match it.

Affirmation:

My abundance mindset is as strong as I choose to make it.

Day 238

A man paints with his brains and not with his hands.

- Michelangelo

Michelangelo's words offer a great analogy for your level of abundance and success. Just as a masterpiece work of art first comes from the artist's mind, so does your own perception of reality. With every thought you think, you are painting a picture of your physical reality. Thinking about your life in this way can be helpful because you start to see that you have full creative control over your life circumstances.

Anything you don't like can be changed – just as an artist can repaint a canvas and change the picture to anything he likes. However, remember that an artist does not paint an entire picture with one large brush; he uses many smaller brushes, many different colors, and thousands of individual brush strokes, which all combine to create the final picture. Your thoughts are exactly the same - just one thought cannot change everything on its own, but many thoughts together can create much bigger changes.

Affirmation:

Every thought I think contributes to the picture of my life.

Day 239

If you don't have time to do it right, when will you have time to do it over?

- John Wooden

John Wooden offers a great insight into the wisdom of doing something right the first time, even if you feel resistant to doing so at first. As he points out, if you don't have the time or energy to do it right the first time you'll just have to do it over again later, probably expending even more time and energy than you would have initially. This concept can be applied to your level of abundance too because if getting your thoughts in order seems like too much effort, you will simply continue creating more of what you don't want – financial lack and struggle.

It makes more sense to take the time to do it right the first time by setting aside adequate time to meditate, visualize, and steadily create the life you truly want. With just a few minutes of your time and energy invested each day, you can begin crafting a life filled with as much abundance, joy, love, peace and happiness as you desire. Yes, it will require effort, but putting forth that effort will be less intensive than trying to fix the damage caused by negative thinking later on.

Affirmation:

I gladly invest the time and energy needed to create my abundant life.

Day 240

It is a miserable state of mind to have few things to desire, and many things to fear.

- Francis Bacon

It's hard to say why the human mind tends to gravitate toward the negative, obsess over negative possibilities, and dwell on the things we least want to experience. Probably a large culprit in this process is habit. We get used to focusing on situations that anger us, upset us or worry us – perhaps because we believe that by doing so we can change them, but that rarely works. The good news is that with a little bit of effort we can also create a positive thought habit.

We can train our minds to always seek the positive possibilities, and focus obsessively on them. No matter how insurmountable challenges appear at first glance, we can shrug and say, "I'll find a way to get around this blockage; I always do." And that belief will attract the very resources we need to breeze through the obstacle. If you have not yet trained your mind to be this positive and confident, start working on it today. All it takes is a continuous conscious choice to focus on the positive outcomes you want – and a refusal to focus on your fears.

Affirmation:

Every time I consciously choose to focus on the positive, my mind gets stronger.

Day 241

Life isn't about finding yourself. Life is about creating yourself.

- George Bernard Shaw

One of the most empowering insights you can internalize is the truth that you can create any version of yourself that you desire. Right now it may seem as though most of your life experiences are out of your control, and in fact your own persona is out of your control because your experiences have shaped who you are. But . . . what if it works the other way around? What if your life experiences are due to the perception you have of yourself as a person?

What if, by changing who you perceive yourself to be, you can also dramatically alter your life circumstances? Take a few minutes today to think about the conditions you are trying to manifest – whether they include having more money, a better job, a bigger house – and then think about the "you" that would come along with those circumstances. Would you be happier, stronger, more confident? Begin trying on that persona for a short time each day and your outer circumstances should gradually start shifting to match it.

Affirmation:

I can be the wealthy, successful, happy person I dream of being.

Day 242

I will love the light for it shows me the way, yet I will endure the darkness because it shows me the stars.

- Og Mandino

As you work on attracting greater abundance into your life, you may sometimes feel as if it's taking forever to get here. Even if you have seen little blips of improvement along the way, you may still be waiting for the bigger manifestations that you really want. It's important not to dwell on feelings of impatience while you wait because they will only delay your progress more.

As Og Mandino suggests above, you can instead find something good about "the darkness" (which could be compared to challenging or difficult life circumstances) and focus on that. Think about your current situation and find one or more things that you can appreciate. It may be something small or it may be something that really thrills you – either way it will keep you focused on the positive, which will help open the floodgates for your greater abundance.

Affirmation:

No matter how dark it gets, I can always find one star to focus upon.

Day 243

I never did a day's work in my life. It was all fun.

- Thomas Edison

Thomas Edison's inspiring quote offers excellent insight about the importance of loving what you do. Even if your current job or business isn't connected to your deepest passions, you can still find plenty of ways to make it fun. You can come up with silly games to get motivated, reward yourself with fun activities after your work is finished, or even write a list of qualities you love about your job or business. Why would you want to do all this?

Because the more you dislike something, the more resistance you create in connection to it, and the less progress you will experience in that area. If you are trying to manifest a better job, your feelings of dissatisfaction for your current job will not be in alignment with the better job you seek. Whatever you focus on the most will keep manifesting in your future experiences, so you will do well finding plenty of ways to focus on fun, success, abundance, and satisfaction.

Affirmation:

By changing my attitude I can make any activity fun and satisfying.

Day 244

Study nature, love nature, stay close to nature. It will never fail you.

- Frank Lloyd Wright

Spending time in nature is a fantastic way to keep your thoughts focused on abundance and happiness. No matter where you live, you probably have some type of natural setting that you can use to calm your mind, relax your body and recharge your positive focus on abundance. Beaches, deserts, mountains, forests, even public gardens – these places are full of inspiring expressions of abundance in the form of vegetation, animals, insects, and more.

As you spend time in these places regularly, you automatically tune into the very essence of abundance and keep your focus on it. The more you focus your attention on abundance, the more you will keep drawing it toward yourself in many different forms. Even better, spending time in natural settings makes you feel calm and peaceful, which means you can release the resistance that may block your greater abundance from arriving.

Affirmation:

Natural forms of abundance are all around me.

Day 245

To get what you want, you have to feel that you already have it.

- Peggy McColl

Peggy McColl's statement above reveals one of the biggest keys to deliberate creation: feel as if you already have the things you want. As simple as this may sound, it's not always easy to do. How can you feel as if you have what you want when you don't really have it? One of the best ways is by using your imagination. Simply set aside some quiet time for yourself, sit or lie comfortably and slip into a fantasy world where you have plenty of money, time, joy, happiness, love, and everything else you desire.

What if you aren't sure what it feels like to have these things? After all, if you've never actually experienced them, how would you know? Pretend! How do you think you would feel if you did have millions of dollars in the bank right now? Would you feel excited? Happy? Elated? Free? Focus on these feelings the best you can, and you will be radiating them to the universe – and the universe will begin reflecting back the experiences that will correspond with your feelings.

Affirmation:

Imagining that I already have the things I want makes me feel good.

Day 246

I not only use all the brains that I have, but all that I can borrow.

- Woodrow Wilson

Have you ever wanted to accomplish something but didn't know how? Are you currently in such a position now? Today's quote by former U.S. President Woodrow Wilson shares wisdom that you can use to accomplish your own life goals – borrow the insight and knowledge of other people. Rather than struggling to find the answers on your own, why not ask the advice of someone you trust? It may be your boss, an associate, friend, neighbor or family member – but try to choose someone who is supportive and encouraging.

If there is no one you can ask in your immediate circle of family and friends, seek insight that may be contained in books, seminars, websites and other media. Has anyone in history already accomplished your goal in one form or another? If so, study what they did and how they did it. Read their biography or study their life history. When you begin actively seeking knowledge and insight like this, you inevitably find it.

Affirmation:

All of the answers I seek come to me easily today.

Day 247

Human beings, by changing the inner attitudes of their minds, can change the outer aspects of their lives.

- William James

Even if you consistently strive to improve your thoughts, you may not yet have improved upon your dominant attitude. One good way to tell if your attitude may be causing problems for you is to consider how you feel when you first wake up in the mornings. Do you feel inspired, eager to start your day, and excited about the good things that will be happening for you? Or – do you awaken with a sense of dread, anger, frustration, sadness or other negative qualities?

If the latter description matches your mindset more closely than the former, you may need to work on turning that around by deliberately thinking more positive thoughts when you first wake up: "I choose to feel optimistic and eager. I know that good things will happen to me today. I choose to feel happy and abundant today!" You can also repeat this process right before bed each evening, and over time you will plant positive suggestions to gradually transform your entire attitude to a very positive one.

Affirmation:

My positive attitude creates my joyful, abundant life.

Day 248

Everything becomes a little different as soon as it is spoken out loud.

- Hermann Hesse

For centuries spiritual teachers have known the power of the spoken word. In a Law of Attraction context, speaking something aloud makes it seem much more tangible and "real". This is important to remember especially when it comes to complaints and other negative statements. By complaining about something – or even verbalizing a negative expectation – you are in essence infusing a thought with physical energy and releasing it into your physical environment, which helps it to manifest much more quickly.

For this reason, you may want to avoid complaining and verbalizing anything negative that you do not want to manifest. Even better, develop a strong habit of constantly verbalizing the good things you do want to manifest. Verbalize your enjoyment of all good things; verbally assert your positive expectations in every situation; and recite your affirmations aloud to help them manifest in full living color in your physical surroundings.

Affirmation:

My voice lends power to my positive intentions.

Day 249

Take chances, make mistakes. That's how you grow. Pain nourishes your courage. You have to fail in order to practice being brave.

- Mary Tyler Moore

When you attempt to manifest greater abundance in your life, there are two ways to go about it: start small and gradually work your way up, or start with the biggest goal you can imagine. Neither way is better than the other, but you may want to consider whether you are purposely holding yourself back from attempting bigger manifestation goals because you fear failure.

You may be setting smaller goals because you wouldn't be too disappointed if they don't work out —but the problem with doing this is that sometimes the smaller goals don't inspire you enough so you don't put forth the effort needed to achieve them. On the other hand, if you are willing to go for the bigger goals, and you are also willing to "fail" as you go along, you will strengthen your confidence to the point where failure becomes a non-issue.

Affirmation:

Little failures move me closer to the bigger success I desire.

Day 250

Always bear in mind that your own resolution to succeed is more important than any other.

- Abraham Lincoln

How determined are you to create the abundant life you desire? The thing about manifestation is that you must be committed enough to consistently work on changing your thoughts, dissolving limiting beliefs and forming positive expectations. If you aren't motivated enough or determined enough to create long-lasting changes, you simply won't devote yourself to the process and nothing much will change. Luckily, there are many ways to develop the motivation and determination to stick with it.

You can dream about the type of life you want to be living in the future and let those images inspire you; look at the things you don't enjoy in your current environment and use them as a stepping stone to imagine even better things. Or you can study the lives of people you admire and pick and choose things from their lifestyles that you would also like to include in your own. Any way you do it, you will be strengthening your own conviction that you deserve better and intend to have it.

Affirmation:

I am fully committed to creating the life of my dreams.

Day 251

Never feel self-pity, the most destructive emotion there is. How awful to be caught up in the terrible squirrel cage of self.

- Millicent Fenwick

Just about everyone on the planet has thrown a "pity party" for themselves at one time or another, but some of us tend to do this to the point that it becomes truly destructive. Especially where the Law of Attraction is concerned, self-pity creates a cycle of negative, debilitating energy that keeps us locked into disempowering situations no matter how badly we would like to escape them.

One good way to overcome this trend is to keep reminding yourself that you always have control over your own thoughts, and by those thoughts you can create positive changes. Whenever feelings of self-pity come up within you, spend a few minutes focusing and reaffirming your spiritual power. Remind yourself that there is no sense feeling sorry for yourself when you could just as easily change your thoughts, take different actions and create an outcome that thrills you.

Affirmation:

I choose to empower myself in every situation.

Day 252

What we call the beginning is often the end. And to make an end is to make a beginning. The end is where we start from.

- T.S. Eliot

As T.S. Eliot reveals in his quote above, an ending is merely another beginning. Keeping this in mind as you work on attracting more abundance can be helpful because you may have noticed that your progress seems to come in waves at first. You may enjoy a short period of increased abundance for awhile but before you know it the abundance slows or stops and you are once again immersed in a pool of lack. You may think that you have failed at this point, but nothing could be further from the truth. Instead, try to see these periods not as endings but as new beginnings – and use them as opportunities to clear your mind, double your efforts and start fresh with greater clarity.

The more you do this the more proficient you become at deliberately calling forth abundance into your life, and the less turbulent the "ocean of abundance" will seem to be. Even better, when you treat these stopping points as no big deal, they can usher in bigger opportunities even faster than they would if you fought and struggled and resisted them.

Affirmation:

Each and every moment, I start fresh in attracting abundance.

Day 253

Very little is needed to make a happy life; it is all within yourself, in your way of thinking.

- Marcus Aurelius

Doesn't it seem sometimes like you have a very long way to go before you reach your financial goals? You have a certain amount of abundance now, and you crave a much larger amount of abundance before you will feel satisfied and happy – but Marcus Aurelius offers a great reminder that you don't have to wait until you have reached your financial goals to feel happy.

In fact, the happier you can get right now, the more easily you will draw more abundance into your life. Even better, you don't have to be happy with every part of your life exactly the way it is now. All you have to do is find one or two things that you can feel happy about, and that focus on satisfaction, happiness and gratitude will be enough to transform the other areas too.

Affirmation:

I love to direct my thoughts to happy things.

Day 254

None are so old as those who have outlived enthusiasm.

- Henry David Thoreau

It's easy to forget sometimes that enthusiasm has a lot to do with your level of abundance in life. In fact, if you think about it, the polar opposites of enthusiasm would be feelings like boredom, disinterest and frustration – which are all the equivalent of stagnation, and abundance cannot thrive in stagnant conditions. Abundance is free-flowing, vibrant energy that needs a lively environment to thrive.

How lively is your environment? If it needs a little perking up, you might try going on a cleaning and organizing spree. Put on some upbeat music then clear away clutter, sweep out the cobwebs and open the windows to clear the air. You can also create a new enthusiasm habit by making time each day for activities that stimulate you mentally, emotionally and physically. Learn something new, watch exciting action movies, exercise – get your own energy flowing and you will become more receptive to the energy of abundance too.

Affirmation:

I deliberately seek activities that make me feel enthusiastic.

Day 255

With the new day comes new strength and new thoughts.

- Eleanor Roosevelt

How do you start most of your days? Do you wake up, shuffle to the shower, then mindlessly go on with your normal routine? Or do you take time to deliberately focus your thoughts and set a positive tone for the day? You may be surprised at the difference such an activity can make in your life if you've never tried it before. If you'd like to start, get yourself a nice notebook and a pen, and keep them in a convenient place to do a bit of writing when you first wake up.

When you wake up the next morning, start by writing, "Today I intend . . ." and fill in the details about the kind of day you'd like to have, any specific experiences you would like to have, solutions to problems you would like to receive, and so on. Spending as little as 5 or 10 minutes focusing on these positive possibilities will boost your mood and leave you feeling inspired – which can help attract more positive outcomes in all areas of your life.

Affirmation:

I make time to focus my mind on positive possibilities.

Day 256

Nothing is so exhausting as indecision, and nothing is so futile.

- Bertrand Russell

One of the more challenging aspects of financial difficulty is the way it makes you feel powerless and confused; which prevents you from recognizing possible solutions. Overcoming this obstacle is easier if you start by focusing on any solution at all, even if it doesn't seem very likely to occur. For example, if you were short on money to cover your expenses but couldn't see any possible way to receive more money, you could create an imaginary scenario where you received an unexpected check in the mail for the exact amount you need.

Even if you don't know anyone who would send you money unexpectedly, just by focusing your thoughts on that one possibility (it is a possibility, no matter how unlikely) you open the door to other possibilities too. However, the key in making this work is to engage your emotions and get excited about the imaginary scenario – just as if it were really happening right now. Doing so instantly makes you receptive to the energy of other solutions that would be just as effective.

Affirmation:

By focusing on one possible solution, I invite many more.

Day 257

Our attitude toward life determines life's attitude towards us.

- Earl Nightingale

Have you ever considered that your general attitude about life may be holding back some of the things you are trying to attract? For example, do you often have the perception that life is hard? That nothing comes easily? That there isn't enough to go around so you have to settle for what you have? Very often these types of attitudes are the result of early conditioning and you may not even be aware of them consciously. However, they often reveal themselves when you are in the midst of hardship.

Think about the last time you faced a big challenge, felt overwhelmed by something, or experienced a setback. What was your reaction? What kinds of statements escaped your mouth? Those are big clues as to your general attitude toward life. And changing self-defeating attitudes like these can be accomplished by consistently affirming a positive outlook – like life is as easy as you expect it to be; there is plenty for everyone, and so on. Keep affirming these things until you believe them and your old defeatist attitudes will fade away.

Affirmation:

An attitude is nothing more than a habit of thought.

Day 258

Life can only be understood backwards; but it must be lived forwards.

- Soren Kierkegaard

Have you ever wished you could go back in time and do things differently? Do you ever wonder where you would be today if you had made different choices in the past? As tempting as it may be to focus on these regrets from time to time, they attract only corresponding disappointments. However, you can use the power of regret in a positive way by looking forward into the next few years of your life and considering what you will look back and wish you had done right now.

Will you wish that you had gone back to school to get your degree? Will you wish that you had devoted more time and energy to transforming your thoughts and attracting greater abundance? Will you wish that you had started that business, written that novel, lost weight, gotten into better shape . ..? Start working on these things now. And in a few years, when you look back you'll feel nothing but joy and satisfaction for all you have accomplished.

Affirmation:

I appreciate my ability to work steadily toward my goals.

Day 259

Most of the successful people I've known are the ones who do more listening than talking.

- Bernard M. Baruch

You may be aware of the importance of being a good listener when it comes to your relationships with others, but did you also know that the same skill can help you to manifest more abundance in your life? You can do that by getting into the habit of "listening" for universal guidance every day. If you have been visualizing, affirming and scripting the abundant life you wish to have, the universe is already aware of your desires but may be waiting for you to accept guidance about how to actualize them.

Every morning or evening (or both), set aside a few minutes to sit quietly with a pen and pad of paper nearby. Close your eyes, quiet your mind and ask the universe for solutions to the issues and circumstances you wish to transform. Phrase your questions like this: "Is there anything I can do to make this situation better? What do I need to know about this situation? Am I holding back progress and if so, how?" Listen closely and insights and solutions may come to you.

Affirmation:

My mind is calm and open to universal guidance.

Day 260

The discipline of writing something down is the first step toward making it happen.

- Lee Iacocca

The practice of writing down your goals, dreams, intentions and affirmations can benefit you greatly as you use the Law of Attraction to create an abundant life. One of the reasons why writing them down works so well is because your thoughts move at such a fast pace that it's hard to concentrate on any one thing for more than a few seconds before your mind is zipping off to the next thought. When you write something down, you must focus on it for a little bit longer which helps you tune into the essence of it, so to speak.

To harness this power, try writing down all of the details of the things you want to create in your life. Spend a few minutes on it each day. You can write out your affirmations, keep a gratitude journal, or simply detail your goals and dreams. As Mr. Iacocca suggests, discipline is necessary. You can't do the exercise just once and expect results from it. Instead, work on it regularly and notice how your dreams eventually seem much clearer and stronger.

Affirmation:

Writing my thoughts down gives them power.

Day 261

What we have once enjoyed we can never lose. All that we love deeply becomes a part of us.

- Helen Keller

During the course of your journey as a deliberate creator, you will undoubtedly encounter many "endings," where circumstances, people and places may be removed from your experience in order to make room for even better circumstances. When this happens, you may be tempted to think that you have done something wrong or the Law of Attraction isn't working the way it should, but that kind of reaction will usually just make things worse.

Instead, if you keep in mind that the universe knows much more about the big picture of your life than you do, you can face these moments of uncertainty with complete trust and faith that everything will work out for your highest good in the end. Focus as much as you can on your appreciation for these people, places and things being part of your life at all and you will communicate to the universe that you are ready for even better people, places and things to start making their way into your reality now.

Affirmation:

I so much appreciate everything that is or has been part of my life.

Day 262

You've got to get to the stage in life where going for it is more important than winning or losing.

- Arthur Ashe

One of the biggest reasons people often procrastinate on their manifestation exercises is because they fear failure. They want to improve their lives but they're afraid to try because they'll be crushed by disappointment if it doesn't work out. Manifestation, just like any other goal or new habit, requires consistent practice before progress can happen. Arthur Ashe's wise words above reveal a great technique for overcoming this fear of failure; by placing more emphasis on the importance of "going for it" rather than winning or losing.

If you sometimes resist doing your manifestation exercises because you're afraid you might be wasting your time, try telling yourself that it's just for practice and it doesn't matter if anything comes from the activities themselves. Very often this relaxed approach will be enough to inspire you to move forward, give your best effort, and probably receive a better outcome than you expected – all because you were willing to go for it despite the possibility of failure.

Affirmation:

I'm proud of my willingness to keep moving forward no matter what.

Day 263

Keep your fears to yourself, but share your inspiration with others.

– Robert Louis Stevenson

One of the hardest parts of improving your thought habits is the necessity of no longer allowing fear to rule your mind. Even worse than thinking fearful thoughts, however, is speaking them aloud and spreading them to others. As you do so, other people simply add their own fearful thoughts and reflect them (now magnified) right back to you. It works the same way with complaints and negativity in any form.

To avoid creating this destructive trend in your own life, make a promise to yourself never to speak aloud your fears, worries, concerns or complaints. That doesn't mean you'll never have thoughts along those lines – but when you do, you will instantly turn your attention away from them and instead focus on something positive and constructive. Not only will this benefit you by improving your outlook, it will benefit others by making you a supportive, positive, upbeat person they will enjoy spending time with.

Affirmation:

I spread only joy, love and kindness to others.

Day 264

Write it on your heart that every day is the best day in the year.

- Ralph Waldo Emerson

Can you remember the last time you felt that a particular day was the best day in the year? For most of us those amazing days are reserved for very special occasions, like the day we got married, graduated from college, gave birth to children, and so on. But what if, as Ralph Waldo Emerson suggests, we could hold a perception that every day is a fantastic day? Believe it or not, for most of us it would only require an improvement in our self-talk. Self-talk is one of the things that dictate our mood at any given moment.

If we keep telling ourselves how happy we are, how good we feel, how blessed we are, that this is the greatest day ever we will begin to actually feel that way. And as we feel that way, our outer world will start to reflect it with many wonderful experiences coming our way. It may be hard to believe, but give it a try the next time you want to have a really great day   you just may be surprised by how well it works.

Affirmation:

Today is going to be the best day ever!

Day 265

To succeed . . . you need to find something to hold on to, something to motivate you, something to inspire you.

- Tony Dorsett

One of the easiest ways to attract positive life changes is to keep attuning to the essence of the outcomes you desire. As Tony Dorsett suggests above, it's the surest way to success. Take a moment to think about the outcome(s) you wish to create in your own life. How much money would you like to have? What kind of job or business would make you feel inspired? Where would you like to live; what would your dream home look and feel like?

As you clarify and refine these images in your mind, you will be steadily attuning to the essence of such outcomes and start drawing them into your life. Your beliefs must also be aligned with each outcome, which requires believing that it is possible for you and that you deserve to have it. Can you see the beauty of the partnership between mind and emotions? Your feelings of inspiration and excitement get the energy flowing toward your chosen outcome and your beliefs are the gatekeepers that allow the final results . . . or block them.

Affirmation:

My enthusiasm and my beliefs work together to manifest my dreams.

Day 266

Bad habits are like chains that are too light to feel until they are too heavy to carry.

- Warren Buffet

Warren Buffet's insight above could just as easily pertain to the restrictive nature of limiting beliefs. Limiting beliefs are unnoticeable to most of us and only become obvious when we attempt to move beyond them. Suddenly they become as heavy and binding as chains that restrict our movement. When it comes to attracting abundance, limiting beliefs have the power to keep you locked in endless cycles of lack and scarcity.

Breaking free from these chains is as simple as gradually expanding your beliefs so that they no longer limit you. For example, if you had a limiting belief that you are only capable of earning a certain amount of money, you could keep chipping away at that belief by looking for evidence that contradicts the "truth" of it. Seek out stories about people who overcame such a limitation themselves, or write a list of reasons why you could earn more than that amount of money. The more you can discredit limiting beliefs, the less power they will have over your life.

Affirmation:

I can dissolve limiting beliefs by expanding my perception.

Day 267

Instead of thinking about where you are, think about where you want to be. It takes twenty years of hard work to become an overnight success.

- Diana Rankin

Diana Rankin shares one of the most powerful secrets of deliberate creation: thinking about where you want to be – in other words, focusing on the outcome you want to achieve rather than getting mired in the struggles and problems you are facing right now. This may not always be an easy feat to accomplish because your circumstances might be overwhelming, frustrating and taxing on every level.

However, it gets easier when you remember that you have the ability to selectively focus on whatever you want. Just because a certain situation is happening in your life doesn't mean you have to give it all of your attention. Practice turning your attention away from situations that make you feel powerless or frightened. Instead, focus more of your attention on situations, ideas and possibilities that make you feel inspired and empowered. As your focus on the positive gets stronger, you should notice the unpleasant situations diminishing in intensity.

Affirmation:

I have the ability and the right to choose what I focus on.

Day 268

What this power is, I cannot say. All I know is that it exists...and it becomes available only when you are in that state of mind in which you know EXACTLY what you want...and are fully determined not to quit until you get it.

-Alexander Graham Bell

Alexander Graham Bell could very well be referring to the power of intention with his statement above. When you set a firm intention to achieve something, all of your creative power rises up and begins flowing toward that exact outcome. The universe then responds by orchestrating events, people, resources and opportunities to help you achieve your chosen outcome. But problems arise when doubt, disbelief and uncertainty get in the way.

Doubt, disbelief and uncertainty act as counter-intentions that conflict with your main intention. You cannot intend abundance while also intending lack or struggle at the same time – and make no mistake about it, worry, doubt and fear are perceived as intentions by the universe. Avoiding counter intentions like these is as simple as making sure that you keep more of your attention on abundance than you do on lack. Focus only on what you want, intend with all of your power that it will be your reality, and the universe will respond as if it were your ironclad truth.

Affirmation:

Each thought I think is perceived by the universe as an intention.

Day 269

A man dies daily, only to be reborn in the morning, bigger, better and wiser.

- Emmett Fox

One of the greatest joys in deliberately creating your life with the Law of Attraction is the ability to start fresh, no matter what your life is like right now. If you currently find yourself without enough money, stuck in a job you don't like, in a relationship that isn't working the way you think it should, or any other unpleasant situation, you can change all of it by simply getting clear about what you really want.

To do this effectively, you need to first acknowledge that you have the ability to create virtually anything you want to experience in every area of your life. Then you have to decide what would make you most happy in each of those areas, and start focusing intently on those outcomes. From there you will be led to the means and resources that will help you manifest them in physical form. In this way, deliberate creation is like a powerful process of rebirth that you have at your disposal every single day – but you are the only one who can activate it in your life.

Affirmation:

I can recreate all areas of my life to be joyful and abundant.

Day 270

When defeat comes, accept it as a signal that your plans are not sound, rebuild those plans, and set sail once more toward your coveted goal.

- Napoleon Hill

Along the path of deliberate creation, you may experience moments of defeat – or they will seem like defeat at first glance. For example, you may be putting all of your effort into creating more abundance and success in your life, but you keep experiencing moments of financial frustration. Or you may be working toward a specific goal but see little outer progress happening at all. Moments like these can make you feel like giving up, but Napoleon Hill offers a better approach – see the obstacles as a signal that your plans may need some work.

You may be trying to make things happen in a certain way rather than allowing the universe to orchestrate the outcome for you. Or you may be getting sidetracked by limiting beliefs and need to spend more time transforming them into empowering beliefs. Or you may simply need to be more patient, especially if you have just begun working toward your current goals. By reviewing your recent thoughts, beliefs and actions, you'll become aware of the causes for obstacles and be able to clear them more easily.

Affirmation:

Defeat is an illusion, just like any other obstacle.

Day 271

You have powers you never dreamed of. You can do things you never thought you could do. There are no limitations in what you can do except the limitations of your own mind.

- Darwin P. Kingsley

Have you ever considered just how limiting some of your beliefs really are? It's not just the bigger limitations that can hold you back; the seemingly small beliefs can create many more problems in your life because most often you don't even question them. For example, if you had a desire to start your own business, immediately your mind pours out all of the reasons why you couldn't or shouldn't do it. "But the economy is bad; but I'm not educated enough; but I'm a woman; but banks would never lend money to me" . . . on and on the "buts" (limitations) go.

But what if these things don't have to be true? What if you could train your mind to be open to the possibilities and pursue your dreams anyway? All it takes is a willingness to question these "buts" as they pop up in your mind, and decide that maybe they're not true after all. When you do this, you instantly begin drawing forth the opportunities and resources that will allow you to achieve the goal despite any perceived limitations that otherwise would have been definite obstacles.

Affirmation:

Limitations can only stop me if I allow them to.

Day 272

Stay committed to your decisions, but stay flexible in your approach.

- Tony Robbins

Tony Robbins offers a great suggestion above that can also be applied to the manifestation of abundance – stay committed to the outcome you want, but be open to allowing it to happen in unexpected ways. Most of us do the opposite; we decide on the outcome we want and get attached to having it happen in a very specific way because we believe that would be the best or most convenient (or even the most plausible) way for it to unfold.

But anyone who has used the Law of Attraction deliberately for some time knows that the universe usually has plenty of surprises up its sleeve. Events and circumstances have a way of shifting around so that the most amazing things can happen – things you never would have expected in a million years. By trying to control the unfolding of the whole process, you prevent these miracles from happening and block the most profound and welcome changes from occurring in your life.

Affirmation:

I am willing to let go and stay open to miracles.

Day 273

Always look at what you have left. Never look at what you have lost.

- Robert H. Schuller

Robert Schuller's suggestion is great advice for the way you view abundance in your life. One of the biggest challenges many people face is feeling anxious about spending money, donating money, paying bills, and otherwise expending some of the financial resources they have available. When they don't seem to have enough they feel like they should hold on a little tighter to what they do have, just in case. But doing this broadcasts a message of scarcity to the universe, which can only attract back more scarcity.

Have you done this too? A better approach might be to pay the bills you need to pay, buy the things you must buy, but at the same time keep affirming that you always have more than enough and the universe will provide whatever else you need. It takes practice and a certain measure of faith to truly embrace this mind-set, but astounding things can happen when you finally do. Your money may seem to stretch further, or more money can flow in surprising and unexpected ways . . . but first you must stop clinging in fear to the abundance you already have.

Affirmation:

As I keep emphasizing how much abundance I have, more comes to me.

Day 274

There are no uninteresting things, only uninterested people.

- Gilbert K. Chesterton

Boredom is one sure way to create stagnation in your life, and this is especially true where money and abundance are concerned. Many people become resigned to the fact that they cannot receive more money than they currently have, so they stop trying and settle into a mundane routine of going to work, paying the bills, and going through the motions each day. If they only knew that the "fact" of having only a set amount of money doesn't have to be true for them at all.

Getting inspired about having more money is one sure way to start attracting it into your life and blast yourself right out of a financial rut. One good way to do this is by keeping a journal filled with written descriptions, photos and goals that you want to accomplish in the next few years. Allow feelings of enthusiasm to take over your body as you write about these things, and you will trigger a steady flow of energy and power that will keep expanding your prosperity.

Affirmation:

When I feel enthusiastic I can't help but attract great experiences.

Day 275

The more you praise and celebrate your life, the more there is in life to celebrate.

- Oprah Winfrey

How often do you "praise and celebrate" anything in your life? Like most people, you probably don't give it much thought except perhaps on major holidays or when something really amazing happens. But the fact is, praising and celebrating anything can attract only good things to you, including a constant flow of vibrant abundance in many different forms. Oprah Winfrey of all people would be able to confirm that!

Praising and celebrating might sound like it requires a lot of effort, but all you really have to do is find positive aspects of the situations, people and places in your life that you can focus on. One positive quality about each of the people you know; one positive aspect about your job; one thing you love about your home or neighborhood or church – keep focused on these positive things and do what you can to celebrate their existence in your life. When you do, you immediately inspire the universe to send you even more things to praise and celebrate.

Affirmation:

Today I will actively look for things to praise and celebrate.

Day 276

You cannot shake hands with a clenched fist.

- Indira Gandhi

The above quote obviously points to peacefulness versus violence, but it also highlights a great point about allowing abundance into your life. When you ask the universe for more money and other forms of abundance, you cannot "clench your fists" and allow it in at the same time. To allow (receive) abundance, your hands and your heart must be open to it.

That means releasing feelings of anger, frustration, tension, and struggle, and transitioning into a more open, relaxed state of mind like peacefulness, joy, gratitude and love. Starting today, begin monitoring your overall state of mind in regards to money and abundance, and notice if you often feel tense and closed like a clenched fist. If so, your number-one focus should be to relax and open yourself to allow abundance to flow more easily.

Affirmation:

When I relax, open, and breathe, abundance flows to me easily.

Day 277

Faith consists in believing when it is beyond the power of reason to believe.

- Voltaire

It is easy to have faith in an abundant future when your life is flowing smoothly and positively, but during times of hardship you may feel overwhelmed by doubt and uncertainty. Yet faith is one of the most powerful tools for change when it comes to using the Law of Attraction deliberately. In fact, faith alone can be enough to call forth some amazing positive changes even when a situation seems to be completely hopeless.

One of the best ways to use faith in your abundance manifesting practice is to get into the habit of embracing uncertainty and using it as a stepping stone to something better. For example, if you feel nervous or worried about money and you don't know how or when things might improve, say aloud frequently: "I don't know how to improve my situation, but I have faith that there are many ways it can happen. I have faith that the universe can show me. I have faith that the right opportunities will show up with perfect timing." Then let go and trust that it is done.

Affirmation:

Faith is the inner light I use to dissolve negativity and fear.

Day 278

Success is a science; if you have the conditions, you get the result.

- Oscar Wilde

Oscar Wilde's insight also pertains to the true power of the Law of Attraction because our entire goal in deliberate creation is creating the right conditions for the abundance and success we desire. What does it mean to create the right conditions? In a manifestation context, it means moving yourself into the state of mind and emotion that you will have once your desires manifest. That means thinking, feeling and acting as if your goal is already a reality.

It can also mean making preparations in your outer world to make room for the physical outcome you desire, like clearing clutter and releasing old relationships, obligations, activities and habits that no longer serve you. The preparations will be different for each person depending on what they want to attract. For yourself, take a look at your life, your habits, and your dominant thoughts and then ask yourself, "Do these things match the outcome I am trying to create?" If not, spend some time creating the right conditions to allow it.

Affirmation:

With clarity and enthusiasm, I make room for abundance in my life.

Day 279

When someone does something good, applaud!
You will make two people happy.

- Samuel Goldwyn

How often do you feel pleased when you see someone else prospering or succeeding? Sadly, most of us spend more time in the grip of that little green envy monster. It's not that we don't want others to succeed, but we feel frustrated that we ourselves are not succeeding as much as others, so it makes us feel like we're lacking in some way, which is never a good feeling.

The good news is that the more we focus on being happy for others' success, the more success and abundance will flow to us. If you often feel resentful about other people's success, you may want to try an experiment for the next few weeks and deliberately celebrate whenever you see someone doing well, succeeding or demonstrating great abundance. Allow your heart to fill with gladness for them and affirm that your own abundance will increase in proportion to the joy you feel for others. This practice can work quickly to boost your own abundance and success.

Affirmation:

Appreciating abundance in any form makes me more abundant!

Day 280

What is told in the ear of a man is often heard 100 miles away.

- Chinese Proverb

The words you speak have a powerful ripple effect throughout your entire life, especially in an energetic context. You may think that complaining to a close friend is harmless – after all, you're just "venting" right? However, every one of those negative words is being actualized in physical form the moment they leave your mouth. In fact, even just thinking those complaints emits energetic signals that communicate your displeasure, frustration and anger.

It's entirely normal to feel frustrated at times; but how you handle that frustration is the key in manifesting better circumstances – or more situations to feel frustrated about. An ideal response to annoyances would be to first acknowledge that the situation is upsetting you, and then immediately start focusing on what you would rather have happen. Decide on some good solutions to turn the situation around and focus on those, thereby attracting more and more solutions and harmony into your life.

Affirmation:

My reaction to negativity can usher in great positive changes.

Day 281

It is awfully important to know what is and what is not your business.

- Gertrude Stein

Gertrude Stein offers a great insight that applies powerfully to the process of attracting abundance or anything else you want, and that is the necessity of not worrying about things that aren't your business. How often have you started the day with great intentions to keep your thoughts focused on the positive, and before you knew it you were reacting angrily to something that someone else did or said, and your good intentions went right out the window? As difficult as it may be at times, it's vital to remember that only your own state of mind is your "business".

Basing your inner peace on the words or actions of other people is a sure way to feel unbalanced and turbulent, which can wreak havoc on your ability to manifest better life circumstances. On the other hand, if you focus more of your attention on your own intention to remain balanced and calm, you instantly empower yourself to transcend outer distractions and stay focused on the outcome you are trying to create.

Affirmation:

I am in charge of my mood and mindset, always.

Day 282

What the mind of man can conceive and believe, it can achieve.

- Napoleon Hill

Napoleon Hill's statement above is undoubtedly one of the most famous quotes relating to the Law of Attraction, but it's easy to skip over the deeper message it holds. Reading the sentence quickly we understand that whatever we can imagine with our minds, we can create. But the part about believing is vital because without belief you won't be able to manifest your desires, no matter how much you think about them.

Instead, what many people do is say to themselves, "I would love to have this outcome, but I can't see any way to make it happen." That element of disbelief will keep blocking the opportunities that would make the goal possible to achieve. One of the most empowering things you can do for yourself is actively keep believing that if you have a dream in your heart, there are endless ways to make it a reality, even if you can't yet see them. Keep believing those ways exist, however, and they will begin to appear in an endless stream of possibilities.

Affirmation:

I believe that my dreams can and will manifest.

Day 283

You will never stub your toe standing still. The faster you go, the more chance there is of stubbing your toe, but the more chance you have of getting somewhere.

- Charles F. Kettering

It takes courage to begin attracting better life circumstances, and sometimes people feel too nervous to actually start working on it. Instead they keep reading and learning about it but never get around to applying the techniques they've learned. Have you done this too? If so, you may want to consider the possibility that you are afraid to "stub your toe" – or fail, in other words. You may have convinced yourself that it's safer to stay where you are, dreaming of a more abundant life without having to face the fear of the unknown and the possibility of failure.

The problem with doing this is that nothing can really change. The remedy to overcome this fear and hesitation is to be willing to stub your toe and acknowledge that you can still make progress even if you stumble now and then. Decide that stubbed toes are no big deal, and not only will they become no big deal, they will probably happen less frequently than they will if you keep fearing them.

Affirmation:

When I stumble, I just pick myself right back up again.

Day 284

A mind always employed is always happy. This is the true secret, the grand recipe, for felicity.

- Thomas Jefferson

Do you ever feel "stuck" in your attempts to attract more abundance, like you are thinking a lot about it but not really getting anywhere? Often this happens because you are unintentionally focusing on lack in one form or another. Either you are noticing your lack of progress (or slow progress) or you are not focusing keenly enough on the abundance you are trying to attract.

One good way to get beyond this stuck feeling is to enter into a state of make-believe to keep your mind busy focusing on abundance. Spend an hour or two pretending that you are already immensely wealthy and feel grateful for it. Draw up some plans for a day of shopping and imagine all of the fun things you will buy. Mentally redecorate your home, or even create your dream home from the ground up. Pretend that you already have the money to afford these things and your feelings of being stuck should dissolve quickly.

Affirmation:

When I focus deliberately on feeling abundant now, abundance must come.

Day 285

Your mind will answer most questions if you learn to relax and wait for the answer.

- William S. Burroughs

One of the greatest gifts in knowing how to use the Law of Attraction is your ability to attract answers and solutions to any problems or challenges you may currently be experiencing. The first step in doing so is to get clear about the essence of the outcome you want to receive. For example, if your problem is inadequate income, the essence of the outcome you wish to receive would be having more than enough money to cover your needs and still have money left over.

Attracting the solution to this problem is as simple as continuing to focus on that essence (more than enough money) and how it makes you feel. Focus on feeling secure, abundant, happy, free – any feelings that having plenty of money would provide for you. The more you focus on these feelings, the more solutions the universe will be able to orchestrate in your life. Once they start appearing, your job is to follow where you are led and take action on the opportunities and insights while holding positive expectations for the outcomes that may result.

Affirmation:

I now expand my awareness to allow solutions to challenges.

Day 286

Imagination is everything. It is the preview of life's coming attractions.

- Albert Einstein

Even if you understand that your thoughts are all-powerful in creating your reality, you may still struggle to make visualization and other abundance-attracting activities a high priority in your life. At the same time you have a burning desire to create some positive changes, your current circumstances may seem too demanding, stressful, and overwhelming, which makes it difficult to find the time to focus on something better.

Albert Einstein's inspiring words above might provide the motivation you need by reminding you that your dominant thoughts are truly the preview of your life's coming attractions. The quality of those attractions depends solely on which kind of thoughts you allow to take over your mind: positive or negative. Even if you have no time for visualization or meditation, making time (even a few minutes a day) will be a powerful, valuable investment into a brighter future.

Affirmation:

I easily make time to dream and imagine every day.

Day 287

A weed is but an unloved flower.

- Ella Wheeler Wilcox

Most of us have situations in our lives that we would consider to be "weeds"; perhaps a difficult relationship, a painful physical condition, and yes, financial lack and struggle. As much as we would love to yank these weeds out permanently, it's important to acknowledge that their very existence can teach us a lot about our counterproductive thought patterns. If you have some of these persistent "weeds" in your life, take a few minutes to jot them down on paper.

Once your list is done, spend a few minutes thinking about each item on it and consider what that situation can teach you. Why is it prevalent in your life? What were the dominant patterns of thought that brought it into being? What can you learn from those patterns and how can you replace that weed with a stunning flower in the future? This exercise should provide insight on chronic thought patterns and clarity about ways to change them in the future.

Affirmation:

I love the weeds in my life for revealing errors in my thinking.

Day 288

You can have anything you want if you want it badly enough. You can be anything you want to be, do anything you set out to accomplish if you hold to that desire with singleness of purpose.

- Abraham Lincoln

Passion, determination and desire are powerful in their ability to draw specific situations and experiences into your life, but President Lincoln forgot to address one vital piece of the puzzle: belief. Wanting something badly and not believing that you can have it is a sure way to end up feeling stuck and frustrated. On the other hand, wanting something badly and believing with your whole heart that you will receive it stimulates powerful feelings of excitement and anticipation. Can you feel the difference between those two attitudes?

The universe picks up on the difference too, and will only deliver that which you believe you can have. If you are currently working on attracting something and you feel uncertain about whether it will come or not, you may want to focus on building a powerful belief that it will be yours no matter what. Say things like this frequently: "I know I will be shown how to achieve this goal; I know I will receive this outcome; I believe this will be my reality," and notice that your energy and intention are amplified and strengthened as a result.

Affirmation:

I choose to believe that everything I desire is possible.

Day 289

If you deliberately plan on being less than you are capable of being, then I warn you that you'll be unhappy for the rest of your life.

- Abraham H. Maslow

Sometimes it's hard to imagine that we can use the Law of Attraction to accomplish virtually anything we desire. Most of us are so used to being stuck in limited thinking that we unintentionally set goals that are less than what we really want – and less than we are capable of achieving. Have you noticed that you do this too? If so, you might enjoy performing an exercise to expand your vision and create some exciting new goals.

Grab a sheet of paper and a pen, and write some ideas on what you would create if you truly knew there were no limits. If you could be anyone you wanted to be, have anything you wanted to have, what would you choose? Once you have a list of ideas, begin working on expanding your belief that you can achieve them. Even if you can't see any possible ways of making them happen yet, affirm that the universe can and will lead you easily to their fulfillment.

Affirmation:

All limits are an illusion.

Day 290

Abundance is not something we acquire. It is something we tune into.

- Wayne Dyer

Wayne Dyer's excellent quote offers a powerful reminder that attracting more abundance isn't what we often perceive it to be. Many of us remain stuck in the illusion that there is only so much abundance in the world and if we don't currently have enough we must obtain more from "out there". But that's not what is really happening when we attract money and abundance. Energetically speaking, we live in a limitless universe that already contains everything we could ever want or need. It is already real and available to us.

Our job is not to go out and obtain more abundance but to bring ourselves into mental and emotional alignment with it so it can flow into our experience. Looking at it this way makes the whole process seem much easier, doesn't it? There is no need to go out and "get" anything – just relax, adjust your thoughts, feelings and beliefs and you will naturally tune into the essence of abundance. And as you tune into it, you automatically allow it to flow easily into your life.

Affirmation:

I tune into abundance by feeling abundant.

Day 291

*Never tell people how to do things. Tell them what
to do and they will surprise you with their ingenuity.*

- General George S. Patton

General Patton's advice also works wonderfully in
the context of attracting abundance. Many people
make the mistake of trying to dictate how the
universe will fulfill their goals and dreams, rather
than letting go and allowing the essence of what
they want to be delivered in the best possible way.
Part of their reason for doing this is that they have
trouble trusting that the universe will deliver what
they really want and they'll get stuck with
something not quite as good. Do you labor under
the same kind of distrust?

If so, you will be glad to know that the universe not
only knows exactly what you want, but can find
endless ways to bring it to you that are fun, exciting
and creative. In fact, the only way you will end up
with something that doesn't please you is if you
continuously keep focusing on what you don't want.
Instead, if you just let go and stay focused on the
final outcome you desire and trust that the universe
can handle it, you'll probably end up with something
much better than you even imagined.

Affirmation:

I trust the universe to deliver my desires in the best
possible way.

Day 292

If you wish to travel far and fast, travel light. Take off all your envies, jealousies, un-forgiveness, selfishness, and fears.

- Glenn Clark

If you haven't yet made as much progress as you'd like with the attraction of greater abundance, you may want to consider the great insight that Glenn Clark offers above. Are you carrying energetic "baggage" that may be preventing you from allowing your abundance to manifest? For example, do you often feel envious of wealthy people? Do you feel jealous when you notice that someone is more successful than you are?

Have you refused to forgive someone for a past betrayal? Do you feel fearful about the changes that increased wealth might create in your life? Believe it or not, these niggling little thoughts in the back of your mind can limit your progress in allowing more abundance – even if your negative thoughts aren't directly related to abundance at all. Do your best to "clean house" energetically and release unnecessary baggage and watch how it can dramatically speed up your progress toward the abundant life you deserve.

Affirmation:

I gladly release everything that interferes with my ability to be abundant.

Day 293

The only limits to the possibilities in your life tomorrow are the "buts" you use today.

- Les Brown

"Buts" can effectively block your attempts to attract more abundance into your life, and it's possible to be under their spell without even realizing it. Have you ever said things like the following statements? "I would love to find a higher paying job but . . ." "I would love to pay down debt but . . ." "I would love to change my life for the better but . . ." Whatever follows those "buts" is not important because they all have one thing in common: they are merely perceptions and beliefs.

The problem is that if you believe them, they must be true. On the other hand, you could just as easily create some "ands" to replace your "buts". "I would love to find a higher paying job AND I believe I can." "I would love to pay down debt AND the universe is going to provide the means to do it." "I would love to change my life for the better AND I have some great ideas on how to do just that." Keep saying things like this and the universe will take you at your word.

Affirmation:

My perception is my truth, and my truth is my reality.

Day 294

Things may come to those who wait but only the things left by those who hustle.

- Abraham Lincoln

When you begin to grasp the full power of the Law of Attraction, you realize that your old perceptions of struggle, worry, and hustle no longer fit in your life. When you really believe that you live in an abundant, limitless universe, there is no need to hurry or strain to get the things you want. Simply adjust your thoughts, line up your beliefs and allow all of the money, love, well-being and happiness you desire to come right to you.

Then your actions will not be motivated by fear but rather by joy, excitement, fun, and creative inspiration. Taking action from these positive states of mind can only bring more great things into your life, and you will find that they come much more easily than when you struggle and fight your way forward. With each and every goal you have, your aim should be to align with the outcome mentally and emotionally, then – and only then – take action from that blissful state.

Affirmation:

I take action easily when I am propelled by enthusiasm.

Day 295

Stop improving. You will be surprised to know that the energy that was involved in improving becomes your dance, your celebration.

- Osho

If you have ever felt frustrated that it seemed to be taking forever to mold and shape your life into what you wanted it to be, you will appreciate today's insightful quote from Osho. Improving your life and working toward goals and dreams undoubtedly requires an investment of substantial energy and focus. What if you could take even a fraction of that energy and instead use it to celebrate the life you already have?

You don't have to stop striving for improvement all together – but rather focus more of your attention on the joy, blessings and abundance that are surrounding you now. When you do this you end up feeling happy, grateful and content with what you already have – but you also instantly begin attracting more and more abundance that will flow into your life in the coming days, weeks, months and years. Celebrate your now, and you will create more to celebrate later.

Affirmation:

I am in love with my present and excited about my future.

Day 296

Don't judge each day by the harvest you reap, but by the seeds you plant.

- Robert Louis Stevenson

People often make a mistake when they are in the beginning stages of attracting more abundance into their lives by looking for the results before they have finished planting more than a few seeds. The problem with doing this is that they may end up feeling discouraged if they haven't given results enough time to show. Have you done this too? One of the best ways to avoid feeling discouraged is to purposely not look for results but focus all of your attention and effort on planting the seeds and having fun while you do it.

In this case, that means visualizing the more abundant lifestyle you wish to have, creating doorways through which abundance can come to you, following inspired actions when you receive them, and so on. Don't worry about whether you're getting results or not – when the results show up you won't be able to help but notice. They will pop right into your life in fun, exciting, rewarding ways. You definitely won't miss them, even if you're not actively looking for them at the time.

Affirmation:

Planting seeds of prosperity is so much fun that I'm not in a hurry to see them bloom.

Day 297

A mind once stretched never returns to its original dimensions.

- Brian Rose

Perhaps you've never considered this before, but all of the work you have been doing to improve your thinking and expand your limiting beliefs will serve you in many, many ways throughout the rest of your life. As Brian Rose suggests above, you cannot ever go back to your old, limited, defeated ways of thinking and living and that is a wonderful thing! From here on you can only keep expanding and growing, including your level of abundance.

You can enhance this process by deliberately saying things like this to yourself often: "Every day I am growing in wisdom and wealth. Every day I expand my vision of what is possible. Every day I feel happier and more abundant. Every day I learn something wonderful about myself." Keep reinforcing the perspective of your life being an amazing journey of growth and evolvement and you will enjoy your unfolding much more.

Affirmation:

Every day I widen the flow of abundance through my life.

Day 298

Be not afraid of growing slowly, be afraid only of standing still.

- Chinese Proverb

Even if your progress is sometimes slower than you would like, keep affirming to yourself that you are definitely not standing still. It may seem that way at times, but there is a good way to tell for sure whether you have made any progress, and that is by considering how you feel. When you have made energetic progress, it will show clearly in your overall emotional state.

Feeling light, happy, clear, optimistic, and excited about what is coming next are all great signs that you are moving forward energetically – and it won't be long before that progress begins manifesting physically too. Even if you occasionally still feel frustrated, defeated or stuck, you probably feel that way less often than you used to. That is also a great sign that progress is happening and it won't be long before the physical signs start showing.

Affirmation:

When I feel good, I know I'm making great energetic progress toward my goals.

Day 299

Nothing in life is to be feared, it is only to be understood.

- Marie Curie

A shortage of money can definitely make you feel fearful and vulnerable, especially if you don't understand how the situation came to be your reality. In fact, if most of your life experiences have carried the stamp of lack, scarcity and struggle you may mistakenly believe that such things are your lot in life, or you are destined to be broke and stressed. Not so! Once you begin to explore the power of your thoughts, you quickly realize that there are very clear reasons for everything you experience.

The tricky part is learning how to set aside your false assumptions, limiting beliefs and fear-based responses so that you can see what is really happening in your thoughts to create such experiences. That can be challenging, but once you get beyond the questions, the answers rise up to meet you. Then it's a simple matter of moving deliberately and steadily to better thoughts, and watching in amazement as your outer life transforms as a result.

Affirmation:

There is an answer for every question, a solution for every problem.

Day 300

If you realized how powerful your thoughts are, you would never think a negative thought.

- Peace Pilgrim

When you fully grasp the power of your thoughts, you may feel a bit intimidated or worried when you catch yourself thinking negative thoughts. However, keep in mind that you must repeatedly think in a certain way over time before your thoughts will manifest. Just like worrying about something for a few minutes won't make it manifest instantly, neither will your negative thoughts about money manifest instantly.

The best thing to do when you notice that your thoughts are veering into negative territory is gently say to yourself, "I don't want to keep following that line of thought because it won't serve me. Instead, I'm going to focus on something that makes me feel happy and grateful." Then call to mind something that does just that – even if it's not related to money and abundance. Doing this consistently will train your mind to stay focused on positive subjects more often than negative.

Affirmation:

My thoughts are powerful, and only I have control over my thoughts.

Day 301

If a window of opportunity appears, don't pull down the shade.

- Tom Peters

Once you start making progress on improving your thoughts regarding money and abundance, you may be presented with an unexpected opportunity – what many of us would call an "inspired action". An inspired action is the universe's way of helping you to make progress physically so you can catch up with your energetic progress. But many people, when they receive these great opportunities, are too afraid to take them.

If this is your experience too, you may find yourself wondering if the opportunity is too good to be true, or worrying that nothing will come of it, and you may be tempted to dismiss it as coincidence, telling yourself it probably wouldn't have worked out anyway. As tempted as you may be to dismiss the opportunities that come your way, don't. Vow to take action in a very detached, relaxed manner and not worry about the outcome. That attitude alone can attract many wonderful opportunities that pay off in countless ways.

Affirmation:

I confidently and boldly pursue opportunities.

Day 302

There is nothing so useless as doing efficiently that which should not be done at all.

- Peter F. Drucker

When it comes to attracting abundance, there are specific activities that are more productive than others. Among the most important activities would be things like deliberately thinking thoughts that are aligned with abundance, practicing the feeling of having plenty of money, and resolutely removing your focus from negative thoughts regarding money and abundance. Of lesser importance would be things like studying, learning and taking action.

These other activities are certainly important, but unless you have consistently worked on your mental state, the results you would receive from these activities would be minimal. Until you have focused your thoughts consistently where they need to be, you won't be aligned with receiving the great results you are striving for. When you focus on the important activities first, the rest comes easily because you are already aligned with the outcomes you desire.

Affirmation:

I consistently focus on the actions that will yield the best results.

Day 303

The worst tempered people I have ever met were those who knew that they were wrong.

- David Letterman

David Letterman's humorous quote raises an important point about your limiting beliefs regarding money. When you touch upon a belief or perception that resonates with your existing beliefs, it will trigger feelings of anger, despair, fear, worry, anxiety or other negativity within you. This is helpful to know because you can easily root out the most limiting or destructive beliefs and begin changing them. Here's a good way to start: Take a sheet of paper and write down a list of statements that you believe to be true about money.

For example: "Money is hard to come by. I deserve to have plenty of money. I never have enough money." Then do the same with statements that you would like to be true about money: "Money comes easily to me. I always have more than enough money." Say each of these statements out loud and you will be able to tell whether you really believe them or not by the way you feel. Then keep affirming the statements that you would like to be true until they start to feel like truth to you. Over time you can change even your most resistant beliefs in this way.

Affirmation:

I decide what is true for me regarding money and everything else.

Day 304

Forget the resolutions. Forget control and discipline... too much work. Instead try experimenting. Go in search of something to fall in love with... something about yourself, your career, your spouse.

- Dale Dauten

Dale Dauten's advice above works wonders in attracting greater abundance into your life also. In fact, if you haven't already discovered this, you surely will soon: the harder you try to make money come into your life, the farther it will seem to move away from you. That doesn't mean you shouldn't attempt to attract abundance at all – just that you should be careful of your mental and emotional attitude while doing so.

As with anything else in life, if you go about it with a relaxed, cheerful, positive attitude, the results will seem to flow easily to you. If you try to make something happen while feeling tense, irritable or fearful, you'll be blocking those great results from arriving. As the quote above states, try experimenting and have fun with it! Find something to fall in love with or feel passionate about and you will become a magnet for money and abundance in all forms.

Affirmation:

When I feel great, great things are magnetically drawn to me.

Day 305

The rock that is an obstacle in the path of one person becomes a stepping stone in the path of another.

- Source Unknown

Do you ever look at the obstacles in your life as reasons why you can't move forward? Many people do this especially pertaining to money. They hold back on pursuing their dreams because they don't have the money to pay for schooling, start a business, move to another location, and so on. But a shortage of money (or any obstacle) does not have to keep you from moving forward. In fact, here is a fun way to turn that obstacle into a stepping stone.

Remove your focus from the obstacle all together, and instead focus on how happy you will feel about the final outcome when you get there. You don't have to pretend that the obstacle doesn't exist, and you don't have to know how to get around it yet. Simply stop focusing on it and stop using it as an excuse. Look beyond it to the completion of your goal and you will attract untold opportunities for clearing that obstacle or helping you to leap right over it.

Affirmation:

I choose not to see obstacles, and they disappear.

Day 306

To the man who only has a hammer in the toolkit, every problem looks like a nail.

- Abraham Maslow

When you've been working on attracting more abundance for a long period of time, you can slip into a routine and keep repeating the same motions over and over again – despite those actions yielding little results. For example, you may have found a technique that seemed to work well at first but over time the results dwindled. The problem might not be that the technique doesn't work, but you may need to employ other tools and techniques to get to the root of the problem.

Finding out which tool would yield the best results is as easy as recognizing the thought patterns at the root of the problem. Through introspection you may notice that you often fear not having enough – not just money but time, attention, love, and so on. Or you may feel like a "victim" in many of your life circumstances, so you keep attracting financial hardship that makes you feel powerless. Once you see the pattern, the solution will be clear and you will know which tool would be best for turning it around

Affirmation:

I recognize unhealthy thought patterns and resolve them easily.

Day 307

Would you like me to give you a formula for success? It's quite simple, really. Double your rate of failure... You're thinking of failure as the enemy of success. But it isn't at all. You can be discouraged by failure -- or you can learn from it. So go ahead and make mistakes. Make all you can. Because, remember that's where you'll find success. On the far side of failure.

- Thomas J. Watson

Today's quote offers a great insight about the power of taking action to keep improving your life. When using the Law of Attraction, it's necessary to give a lot of attention to improving your thoughts and beliefs, since they form the foundation for all of your life circumstances. Once you begin to improve your state of mind, however, you should notice that more and more physical opportunities start coming your way, simply because you are aligned with receiving them.

But if you are still stuck in old patterns of taking action and receiving no discernible results from them, you might hesitate when these great new opportunities come your way. If you feel anxious about moving forward, remember that you don't have to fear failure – ever – because every small stumble and every great fall will only move you closer to the outcome you desire. Even better, taking action from your new and improved positive state of mind will always bring about positive results, even if they weren't exactly what you expected or hoped to receive.

Affirmation: Only great things can come to me when I act with optimism and faith.

Day 308

Life is a great big canvas, and you should throw all the paint you can on it.

- Danny Kaye

Sometimes it can be challenging to break out of limiting belief patterns that you may have had for many years, and frequently you may not even be aware that you are still limiting yourself in various ways. Today's quote offers a great analogy for embracing the essence of joy and possibility in your life and finally breaking free from limiting beliefs for good. If your life was a blank canvas and you could paint anything you wanted upon it, what would you paint?

Most likely you would improve certain situations that already exist – but beyond those smaller initial goals, what would you CREATE? Would the picture of your life be bright, vibrant, and energized; or serene, peaceful, and meaningful? Would it be well-organized and balanced; or crazy, spontaneous and joyful? There are no right or wrong answers – your canvas is yours to paint any way you like. But first you have to be willing to believe that you are the artist in charge, no one else.

Affirmation:

Every thought and every action is a brush stroke on my life canvas.

Day 309

You have within you right now, everything you need to deal with whatever the world can throw at you.

- Brian Tracy

Do you ever feel as if you don't have the strength to handle the challenges that come your way? Especially if many of these challenges are financial, the result can often be feelings of powerlessness and fear. It's important to acknowledge that feeling disempowered or fearful about outer circumstances means that you have lost touch with your inner knowing that you are truly the creator of your life.

To reconnect with this knowing, you need only get quiet and turn your attention inward. Deep inside of you is a wise, loving, all-powerful force that knows you are never incapable of handling anything. Not only can this inner power help you to feel more confident in handling your current life experiences, it can help you to create much better experiences from this point onward. Get into the habit of consulting this inner knowing daily, and you will naturally and easily unleash the confidence, strength and power that was within you all along.

Affirmation:

I am empowered and supported from within.

Day 310

All difficult things have their origin in that which is easy, and great things in that which is small.

- Lao-Tzu

Today's insightful quote offers a great reminder of the simplicity of using the Law of Attraction to improve your financial life, or any aspect of your life. The first part of the quote reminds us that no matter how intimidating or complex a situation may appear to be, it was created easily by one or more negative thoughts relating to it. To unravel a big, snarled mess, you simply have to keep choosing better and better thoughts about it and it will naturally unwind as something better is formed in its place.

The second part of the quote is just as inspiring because it reveals your ability to create great things just by starting small with one or two positive thoughts. Those one or two positive thoughts will keep attracting more and more like themselves, until finally you start building momentum, expanding the idea, flowing more and more energy into it – and magic begins to happen as suddenly you are led to the perfect opportunities to make the dream a reality

Affirmation:

One little thought at a time can build the great life I desire.

Day 311

At first, dreams seem impossible, then improbable, and eventually inevitable.

- Christopher Reeve

When you first conceive a desire and begin working deliberately with the Law of Attraction to achieve it, there is a strong likelihood of getting discouraged if you don't understand the process of manifestation. It's not as simple as just thinking about something occasionally and waiting for it to pop into your life. More often, you will need to undergo an inner journey and gradually align with the essence of your desire.

To attract great wealth, for example, you need to shift your thoughts and beliefs so that you become a person who is already wealthy. Waiting until the money shows up before you can feel wealthy will forever keep the money away from you. Understanding this crucial process of inner "becoming" will greatly help you in your manifesting attempts because at any moment you will be able to tune into how you feel and know just how close you are to the realization of your desire – or how much more transformation is needed before it will happen.

Affirmation:

In every moment I am becoming the person who is living my ideal life.

Day 312

He who asks a question is a fool for a minute; he who does not remains a fool forever.

- Chinese Proverb

Asking questions of yourself is a great way to tap into your intuition and figure out exactly where you may have blockages relating to money and abundance. The proverb above uses the word "fool," which is a bit too strong for our purposes. "Ignorant" might be a better word because ignorance means not being aware of something. If you aren't aware of the cause of your blockages, you will have a much harder time trying to dissolve them.

To consult your intuition, try the following exercise. Sit quietly for a few minutes to quiet your mind and relax your body. Then turn your attention inward to the center of your chest and ask questions like these: "What is my biggest blockage relating to money? What is the most destructive financial habit I have? What can I do to heal my relationship with money?" Then listen for answers and jot them down when you receive them. Most often the answers will come smoothly and quickly, they will be profoundly accurate and easy to put into action.

Affirmation:

My inner wisdom always has the answers I seek.

Day 313

You don't pay the price for success. You enjoy the price for success.

- Zig Ziglar

Many of us have been taught to believe that reaching a state of success in our lives has to be a difficult, strenuous, unpleasant journey. Even once we understand the power of our thoughts and we know that it doesn't have to be so hard, we may still have a hard time releasing the tendency to struggle because we've done it for so long. One good way to overcome this tendency is to keep affirming that becoming successful can be fun and easy.

"I know that success can come easily to me. I am having fun becoming more successful each day. Making my goals fun to work on ensures my success!" Affirmations like these are great tools to gradually change your thinking so that success no longer seems like a difficult achievement. Once you begin to believe it, you will find that working toward your success, and maintaining it later, becomes a natural and automatic process – no struggle necessary.

Affirmation:

I choose the easy, fun route to success.

Day 314

Here's to the happy man: All the world loves a lover.

- Ralph Waldo Emerson

Would you say that you are happy, overall? Or do you feel happy in some ways but unhappy in others, like most people? One of the greatest ways to start drawing more abundance (and all forms of goodness) into your life is to feel happy now. The challenge is: how do you feel happy when there are things in your life that definitely don't make you feel happy? One simple way to start is by focusing on something that does make you feel happy.

You can imagine a future experience and how happy it would make you feel when it happens; or you can focus on something in your current circumstances that is going well; or you can just plain choose to feel happy no matter what else is happening around you. It may sound difficult, but it gets easier every time you do it. Just detach from whatever is bothering you and focus on feeling happy, whatever it takes. Quickly you should notice that your inner happiness is being reflected back to you from outer circumstances – usually in fun and inspiring ways.

Affirmation:

Right now, I choose to let go and feel happy no matter what.

Day 315

You can be pleased with nothing when you are not pleased with yourself.

- Lady Mary Wortley

Self-worth plays a very large role in the creation of your abundant life, but it's a quality that you may not think about very often. A good way to gauge your perception of self-worth is to say some targeted statements like these: "I deserve to be wealthy. I am a good person. The universe loves me and supports me. I deserve to be loved. I deserve to be happy." As you say these statements, you should notice feelings that come up in response to them, and these feelings will be of a positive or negative nature.

Negative feelings like anger, disbelief or guilt are red flags that you do not really believe the words you are saying, which can block your abundance from arriving. To begin strengthening your self-worth, make it a daily habit to speak positively to and about yourself. Affirm that you are a good person, you do deserve to be wealthy and happy, and the universe does love and support you. Consistent practice with these affirmations should steadily improve your feelings about yourself and ease inner resistance, which should allow your abundance to flow.

Affirmation:

I am worthy of every good thing I desire.

Day 316

True silence is the rest of the mind; it is to the spirit what sleep is to the body, nourishment and refreshment.

- William Penn

Sitting in silence is one of the most powerful tools available to you in your process of attracting more abundance. When you sit quietly and allow your mind and body to relax for a few minutes, instantly you begin dissolving energetic resistance that was interfering with your "signal" to the universe. Resistance, at its core, is composed of negative thoughts, scattered or disorganized thoughts, turbulent emotions, stress, confusion, and fatigue.

When you sit in silence and let go of stress and scattered thinking, your energy signal becomes much clearer and stronger. You reconnect with your inner peace and immediately begin attracting more situations in which you will feel peaceful and calm, which can go a long way in improving your outer circumstances. If sitting in complete silence makes you feel too restless, try putting on some soft music or nature sounds in the background. As long as you disconnect from stress and tap into the well of serenity within, you will still make progress.

Affirmation:

No matter how busy my life gets, I make time to connect with my inner peace.

Day 317

You cannot depend on your eyes when your imagination is out of focus.

- Mark Twain

Your perceptions are often based on underlying beliefs that you developed years ago, and those perceptions affect the way you see the world around you. That may not seem like a big deal, but when you consider that you are constantly broadcasting a "signal" to the universe based on the things you see, believe and experience about your life circumstances, it becomes a very big deal. To change the way your world looks, you will need to change the way you see it – and one of the best ways to do that is by using the power of your imagination.

No matter which situations in your life make you feel frustrated, sad, powerless or angry, you can change them by choosing to see them differently. Start with one situation and think about how you would like it to appear to you – and then begin visualizing the situation being that way. Infuse a lot of excitement and happiness into the process and imagine that the situation really has improved and you feel great about it. Do this consistently for a week or two and you should notice that the situation begins transforming to match your new perception of it.

Affirmation:

I can choose to see my life experiences in a better way.

Day 318

The purpose of art is washing the dust of daily life off our souls.

- Pablo Picasso

"The dust of daily life" that Pablo Picasso describes in today's quote could also serve as a symbol for the things that interfere with our ability to attract greater abundance. Boredom, frustration, sadness, fear, stress, powerlessness, and other negative feelings keep us locked in a state of lack, and in that state we are not a match to the essence of abundance.

Viewing beautiful works of art can help lift us out of those negative states – or even better, creating beautiful works of art ourselves! How often do you spend time joyfully creating something? Probably not that often if you are like most people, but it can do wonders for your mood and mindset, and help move you into alignment with true abundance. Don't worry about how "good" your creations are – if they are created with joy they cannot help but be beautiful and beneficial.

Affirmation.

I exercise my creative power daily.

Day 319

Love is the master key which opens the gates of happiness.

- Oliver Wendell Holmes

Love is one of the highest frequency emotions you can experience, and it can be used to transform nearly any situation, including your level of abundance. Take a moment right now to consider how you feel when you are flowing feelings of love toward someone or something. You probably feel light, joyful, happy and passionate, right? Now think about how that high, positive frequency could effortlessly attract more abundance into your life, and you will quickly realize the power of love when applied to abundance.

Focusing on abundance with love is easy to do: simply think about the form of abundance you desire, such as having plenty of money, or a better job, or a bigger home. As you think about it, call up feelings of love from within and direct them toward the image of this object or situation. Say, "I love the thought of having _____ because it makes me feel . . ." and tune into the feelings of having it now. Whatever you desire, love it and it will be drawn to you easily.

Affirmation:

I love abundance in all of its wonderful forms.

Day 320

One generation plants the trees; another gets the shade.

- Chinese Proverb

Today's quote offers a great example of the power of planting seeds of prosperity in your life too – but luckily you don't have to wait years before those seeds sprout and grow! One of the more challenging aspects of attracting abundance is that sometimes it's hard to tell if it's working or not. You may spend days, weeks, even months being diligent about improving your thoughts, but if nothing much is happening on the outside you may think your efforts are wasted.

Just as you shouldn't dig a seed from the earth to see if it's sprouting or not, it's hard to "see" what's happening energetically with your new abundance thoughts until they appear in your physical reality – but there is a good precursor, and that is the way you feel. If you are starting to feel more positive and optimistic about money, if you are starting to worry less and feel happy more, you are absolutely moving in the right direction and it will only be a matter of time until your abundance manifests in full living color in your life.

Affirmation:

My mental and emotional states reveal my pending manifestations.

Day 321

If you don't program yourself, life will program you!

- Les Brown

Do you allow your outer circumstances to affect your state of mind each day? For example, do you awaken in a good mood but quickly descend into aggravation and stress as things start to go wrong for you? When you venture out into the world and encounter people in foul moods, does it automatically shove you into a bad mood too? Deliberately choosing a positive state of mind each day is a powerful exercise that can have a strong impact on your level of abundance too – especially if you frequently feel overwhelmed by negative thoughts and feelings about money.

All that's necessary is the commitment to purposely keep thinking more productive thoughts, such as replacing thoughts like, "I'm so sick of money problems" with thoughts like, "I let go and allow more money to flow easily to me". The more you do it, the easier it gets, and the more powerfully you will see a direct correlation between your dominant thoughts and your outer circumstances.

Affirmation:

I am the only one in control of my thoughts.

Day 322

Whine less, breathe more; talk less, say more; hate less, love more; and all good things are yours.

- Swedish Proverb

Transforming your thoughts from negative to positive can have an amazing effect on all areas of your life, even beyond your financial situation. Certainly having plenty of money is a great result of positive thinking, but what if you could also improve your physical well-being, renew all of your relationships, feel passionate about your work, and enjoy peace of mind much more often than you do now?

The proverb above offers some helpful hints on exactly how to achieve these positive outcomes: whining less (also complaining less) and breathing more is a great way to avoid focusing too much on negativity; talking less while saying more helps you to be sure you are communicating effectively which will definitely improve your relationships; and hating less and loving more is a great way to keep the positive essence of abundance unfolding in your life.

Affirmation:

I infuse everything I think, say and do with positive energy.

Day 323

*That which we persist in doing becomes easier -
not that the nature of the task has changed, but our
ability to do has increased.*

- Ralph Waldo Emerson

Did you know that the majority of people will
automatically avoid a task that seems difficult or
challenging? Most often it's not because they are
afraid of hard work, but rather they doubt their own
ability to do the job well, or finish it at all. Have you
done this too? Ralph Waldo Emerson's words
above remind us that the more we do something,
the easier it will get over time, and this is also true
of attracting abundance.

When you first begin improving your thoughts and
aligning with abundance, an extraordinary amount
of effort seems necessary to make any progress at
all. But little by little it starts to get easier and
before long it's a genuine habit to stay aligned with
abundance and therefore keep attracting more and
more of it into your life. The process didn't become
easier; you just increased your ability to do it easily.

Affirmation:

Each day my ability to attract abundance grows

Day 324

*Good timber does not grow with ease. The
stronger the wind the stronger the trees.*

- Williard Marriott

Do you ever wish you could wave a magic wand
and eliminate situations (or maybe people) who
seem to knock you back into negative thinking? It's
understandable to want to remove sources of
negativity because you probably believe that doing
so would make your journey to abundance much
easier and faster. After all, if you didn't have
anything to distract you from your focus on
abundance, it would probably manifest instantly,
right?

It's important to remember that those negative
people and circumstances are actually serving a
great purpose in your life, and that is by helping you
strengthen your ability to focus. Anyone can focus
on the positive when they are surrounded by only
positive conditions – but it takes a true master of
mental discipline to stay focused on the positive
when everything around them is negative. Give
thanks for outer expressions of negativity, for they
are helping you build a solid foundation of mental
strength that will pay off abundantly later.

Affirmation:

My positive focus grows stronger and steadier each
day.

Day 325

We tend to forget that happiness doesn't come as a result of getting something we don't have, but rather of recognizing and appreciating what we do have.

- Frederick Koenig

One of the fastest ways to start attracting more abundance into your life is by making a concentrated effort to appreciate the abundance you already have on a daily basis. You can do this in numerous ways, like counting your blessings, keeping a gratitude journal, and feeling appreciative whenever money comes to you. However, people often get limited results from these kinds of exercises, simply because they don't engage their emotions strongly enough.

The manifestation process is powerfully amplified when you start feeling truly blessed, grateful and abundant. In order to tap into these strong emotions you may need to "pretend" a bit, like pretending that the unexpected $10.00 check you just received is actually a $1,000.00 check; or paying your bills while pretending that you still have many thousands of dollars left over. Do whatever you have to do to really tap into the emotions of gratitude and appreciation and you will see a huge difference in the results you receive from gratitude exercises.

Affirmation:

I am so grateful for the many blessings in my life!

Day 326

*Men are anxious to improve their circumstances,
but are unwilling to improve themselves; they
therefore remain bound.*

- James Allen

It's hard to remember sometimes that improving
your outer circumstances is not your goal. Instead,
as you improve yourself from within, everything
around you will change to reflect the new person
you have become. What kind of inner
improvements need to take place in order for that to
happen? First and foremost, your thoughts must
be consistently redirected to focus on abundance,
until they begin flowing that way automatically.

Also important is choosing better beliefs to create a
new foundation for your abundant lifestyle; beliefs
about yourself and beliefs about the nature of
abundance. Finally, your actions must line up with
your newfound thought and belief foundation – you
can't act and speak in ways that contradict your
new state of mind. It may seem complicated to get
all of these things working together, but the process
can be easy and natural if you simply work at it little
by little, thought by thought, day by day.

Affirmation:

I am becoming a more abundant person with each
passing day.

Day 327

Everything you are against weakens you.
Everything you are for empowers you.

- Wayne Dyer

Do you ever find yourself resisting or "fighting against" things you don't want? For example, you may have a habit of complaining or arguing when people or events get on your nerves, or you might declare war on unpleasant situations that threaten your happiness and take radical action to try to eliminate them from your life. Needless to say, these actions only exacerbate the problems because the more you focus on them the stronger they get.

A better approach might be focusing intently on the situation or outcome you do want to experience, while turning your attention firmly away from things that tempt you to get angry or upset. Simply do an "about face" when you feel like you might start fighting, complaining or arguing about anything negative, and focus on the alternate situation you prefer to have happen instead. Over time, those negative temptations will fade and eventually disappear completely because you stopped infusing them with your energy.

Affirmation:

I focus only on outcomes and situations that empower me.

Day 328

Life is not a problem to be solved, but a reality to be experienced.

- Soren Kierkegaard

Often when people attempt to attract more abundance into their lives, they do so with the intention to eradicate problems that not having enough money can create. In the back of their minds they may be thinking, "Once I attract enough money, I won't have to deal with this problem anymore, I won't have to struggle and scrape by anymore." This may be true, but trying to use the Law of Attraction to solve a problem only reinforces the reality of the problem.

Have you done this too? A better way is to remove your focus from the problems and instead think about the reality you are eager to experience. Are you eager to know that you have unlimited amounts of money at your disposal? Do you look forward to taking exotic trips, buying nice things, upgrading your residence? Focus on the excitement and joy these thoughts inspire in you and the "problems" of not having enough money will fade farther and farther into the background.

Affirmation:

I focus constantly on the abundant reality I want to experience.

Day 329

Learning never exhausts the mind.

- Leonardo da Vinci

As you learn to work with the Law of Attraction, do you ever feel frustrated that there are endless little facets of deliberate creation, and it could take years to understand them all? More often than not, this feeling of frustration is not caused by the learning itself. As Leonardo da Vinci suggests, learning doesn't exhaust the mind; it invigorates it! Feelings of frustration arise because you are trying too hard to "get it done" – believing that once you absorb all of the knowledge you can, you will finally master the application and feel fully in control of your life.

You may be relieved to know that you don't have to know everything to be proficient at using the Law of Attraction, and you do not have to rush to an imaginary finish line to feel complete. Instead, try to see this journey as a constant, ongoing process of expansion and growth; and with every passing day you will become happier, more abundant and more confident in your creative abilities. Adopting such an outlook will immediately relieve feelings of frustration and make your studies fun and exhilarating.

Affirmation:

I will forever keep growing, expanding and becoming more.

Day 330

If you treat every situation as a life and death matter, you'll die a lot of times.

- Dean Smith

Do you often feel as if achieving your goals is a matter of life and death? Of course your goals are important to you, but if you feel exceedingly attached to them, you may be doing yourself more harm than good. When it comes to using the Law of Attraction, being emotionally attached to anything creates blockages, simply because attachment inserts a strong essence of "need" into your energetic signal.

The more strongly you think you "need" something to happen, the less likely it is to happen because you are reinforcing the fact that it hasn't yet happened! If you catch yourself doing this, there is a very simple solution – let go. Just let go of the outcome you want and be willing to trust that the universe will deliver that or something even better when the time is right. Immediately you will feel that sense of urgency dissipate, and your energetic signal will clear, paving the way for a great outcome every time.

Affirmation:

I let go and stay open to all beneficial outcomes.

Day 331

Happiness is a direction, not a place.

- Sydney J. Harris

One of the greatest skills you can develop is the ability to be happy no matter what else is happening in your life. This is especially true in context with the Law of Attraction, because feelings of happiness dissolve resistant energy, and allow great things to come to you easily. But how can you feel happy when not everything in your life is the way you would like it to be? What if there are things in your life that make you feel downright miserable?

The best way to overcome these challenges is by finding one or more things that do make you feel happy, and focusing the majority of your attention on those. For example, even if your financial situation makes you feel stressed, perhaps your relationships are vibrant and loving. Your career may be going very well, or you may be excited about the singing classes you have just started taking. Focus on whatever is going well for you and feel as happy as you can – and that focus on happiness will spread into every other area of your life too.

Affirmation:

I can be happy right here, right now.

Day 332

The luck of having talent is not enough; one must also have a talent for luck.

- Hector Berlioz

Today's quote includes an intriguing comment about having a "talent for luck". Most people think of luck as something you have, or don't have – maybe even something you are born with or without. But once you understand the power of thoughts and how they impact everything you experience during your lifetime, you start to realize that "luck" is nothing more than being in alignment with all forms of abundance.

When you are energetically aligned with abundance, good things are magnetically drawn to you. You cannot help but attract interesting people, great opportunities, easy access to resources, and much more – everything you desire just finds its way to you, and you have to do little to make that happen. To stay aligned with abundance, all you need to do is focus on abundance, feel abundant, and expect abundance at every turn. That alone will make you seem like the luckiest person on the planet.

Affirmation:

Good luck is nothing more than an expectation of good fortune.

Day 333

An artist cannot fail; it is a success to be one.

- Charles Horton Cooley

Whatever circumstances you are trying to attract with the Law of Attraction can be realized easily if you learn how to "be" the person who would be living in those circumstances. As Mr. Cooley states above, just being an artist (or anything else) makes you a success at it, regardless of specific accomplishments that may be achieved as a result. There are two necessary components to this process: belief and physical expression. Before you can "be" anything you must first believe that you are that thing.

In relation to abundance, you would need to believe that you are already abundant, successful, happy and free from all expressions of lack. Then, you would need to begin acting as if that were your truth. That means turning away from lack-focused actions like worrying, doubting and stressing; and engaging in more abundance-focused actions like feeling happy, blessed and carefree. In a relatively short period of time doing this, you would notice that everything around you starts shifting to reflect your new reality of being a truly abundant person.

Affirmation:

Being abundant means thinking, feeling and acting as if I am abundant.

Day 334

No trumpets sound when the important decisions of our life are made. Destiny is made known silently.

- Agnes De Mille

Today's quote stands as a perfect example of the way we receive inspired actions. Inspired actions are ideas and insights that the universe sends our way to help us achieve our goals. If we dare to take action on these insights, they always usher in some positive changes that will move us one step closer to realizing our goals. The problem is that these inner "nudges" are often subtle enough that we may be tempted to dismiss them.

A good way to enhance your awareness of these inspired actions is to pay close attention to how you feel throughout each day. From time to time, check in with yourself and notice if you are experiencing mental or physical "clues" like feelings of apprehension, tightness in your abdomen, jitters or nervousness, or feelings of excitement and inspiration about an idea you just conceived. These signals are often your intuition speaking to you, and following the positive feelings will usually lead you to a positive outcome.

Affirmation:

I intuitively know when an idea would be beneficial for me.

Day 335

Age wrinkles the body. Quitting wrinkles the soul.

- Douglas MacArthur

Have you ever been tempted to give up on attracting more abundance into your life? If you have received only limited results so far (or perhaps none at all), you may be tempted to think that the Law of Attraction doesn't work and you have no choice but to remain stuck in your current circumstances forever. Nearly everyone experiences these moments of doubt from time to time, but quitting is definitely not the right action to take.

Instead, if you ever find yourself feeling frustrated and exhausted because things just haven't been working in your favor, give yourself permission to take a break. Step back from working toward your goals, visualizing, affirming – whatever actions you normally take when working with the Law of Attraction – and just focus on taking it easy for a few days. Often this is enough to dissolve resistance and renew your enthusiasm, which should also jumpstart some outer progress and help you confirm that your previous efforts were not a waste of time.

Affirmation:

It's okay to take it easy on my journey to abundance.

Day 336

When you cannot get a compliment any other way, pay yourself one.

- Mark Twain

Engaging in positive self-talk is a great way to make yourself feel great, and it can also help you to attract abundance more easily. Many of us are guilty of allowing a constant stream of negative thoughts to flow through our minds, and many of those negative thoughts are directed at ourselves. We say derogatory things to ourselves, like: "I'll never get this right. I'm such a failure. Everyone else seems to have it together, why don't I?" Not surprisingly, these negative comments have a negative impact on our energetic frequency.

Instead, you may find it fun to do as Mark Twain suggests; start paying yourself compliments regularly. Say things like this to yourself often: "I am so talented! I really love myself. I'm proud of how far I have come. I believe in my ability to create any lifestyle I want." The more you say them, the more you will come to believe them, and the more you will come to feel better and better about yourself – and that means you will begin allowing much better outcomes in every area of your life.

Affirmation:

I am really good at deliberate creation!

Day 337

We turn not older with years, but newer every day.

- Emily Dickinson

Emily Dickinson shares a great insight about the power of attitude when it comes to attracting abundance or anything else into your life. Most of us don't stop to think about it very often, but each new day is really a brand-new start that we can turn into any kind of experience we like. Imagine if you could wake up and decide what kind of day you would like to have. "Today I would like to be wildly successful. Today I would like to be amazingly joyful and happy."

As you may have guessed, you can choose to make each day exactly what you wish it to be – but the tricky part is first knowing what you want to experience, and the even trickier part is to believe you can have it. For starters you may find it helpful to simply think about what you would love the most, and then repeat your intention for that all day long: "Today I intend to feel abundant and experience situations that amplify my abundant feelings." It may not change everything in an instant, but it can go a long way in helping you feel like a proactive creator.

Affirmation:

Each day is an opportunity to choose a better reality.

Day 338

Cherish all your happy moments: they make a fine cushion for old age.

- Christopher Morley

If you are like most people, you may tend to focus more on things that are going wrong rather than things that are going right in your life. When it comes to attracting abundance, you may already be aware that this is a destructive action because it only keeps attracting more instances of things going wrong for you. A good way to turn this trend around is to start keeping a journal of everything that is going right for you, especially relating to abundance.

For example, if you were to start recording every positive experience you have each day; when money comes to you unexpectedly; when you receive a surprise discount or rebate; when someone gives you an unexpected gift, and so on – you would automatically start attracting more experiences like these simply because you are keeping a strong focus on them. You can also record "fantasies" for things you would like to have happen, and end up creating some of them the more you focus on them. It's a fun, easy way to shift your focus and get great results.

Affirmation:

The more I focus on the abundance I have, the more it expands.

Day 339

Creativity requires the courage to let go of certainties.

- Erich Fromm

One of the first things you'll learn as you work on attracting more abundance into your life is that few things turn out exactly like you thought they would! While it's possible to use the power of deliberate intention to attract specific situations and opportunities into your life, more often it will be necessary for you to let go of the reins and let the universe work on your behalf. This takes a lot of courage and trust – something that you may resist at first.

It may be helpful to note that your resistance to letting go usually stems from a lack of belief that things will work out beneficially for you – or even a lack of belief that the universe will support you and help you. To overcome this doubt, simply keep affirming that it's okay to let go and trust, because the universe has received every single desire you have expressed, it just needs a little time and room to form them into physical being.

Affirmation:

I let go and trust that abundance and joy are on the way.

Day 340

There are perhaps no days of our childhood we lived so fully as those we spent with a favorite book.

- Marcel Proust

Did you know that reading great books can help you attract more abundance? It's not the book itself, or the reading of it that matters. The same thing can happen when you spend time digging in the garden, creating a pretty pot out of clay, or watching a good movie. When you engage in activities like these – activities that thrill you, inspire you, uplift you, or simply distract you from negativity, you are immediately reducing the amount of "static" in your energetic frequency.

Static really means resistance; contradictory thoughts and feelings that block your desires. Focusing on pleasurable activities distracts you from those negative thoughts, your frequency starts to clear and the universe begins returning more outcomes that match your new, happier frequency. As Marcel Proust says above, we are definitely living more fully during those moments because we are connected to the very essence of life: joy, excitement and awe.

Affirmation:

I give myself permission to connect with joy and awe on a regular basis.

Day 341

Your worth consists in what you are and not in what you have.

- Thomas Edison

Have you ever explored your desire for wealth and questioned why it's so important to you? Beyond the obvious reasons of wanting financial security and physical comforts, what else will great abundance do for you? Will it make you feel more important? Powerful? Peaceful? Purposeful? Exploring your reasons for wanting more abundance is a great way to connect with the very essence of your desire and fulfill it even before more money comes to you.

Whether you are craving a greater feeling of security, freedom, peace, excitement and adventure, or anything else, find ways to inspire those feelings within yourself right now. As you begin emitting the frequency of security, empowerment, freedom, joy, peace, or anything else you desire, the Law of Attraction will start returning corresponding physical situations, which will undoubtedly include increased abundance.

Affirmation:

When I feel as if I have it already, the universe sends it to me.

Day 342

Forget the times of your distress, but never forget what they taught you.

- Herbert Gasser

As much as you would sometimes like to forget the pain and fear of your financial struggles, it would serve you much better to use them as great examples of the true power of your thoughts. Whether most of your financial struggles were in the past or the still exist in the present, do your best to recognize the role your own thoughts played in creating them. The insights and lessons you can receive from this introspection are life-changing.

Once you are aware of negative thought patterns, and once you have recognized how they show up in your surroundings, you will never again create unpleasant conditions by accident. You will notice immediately when your thoughts start moving in that negative direction and you will do what's necessary to firmly move them back to a positive direction. And that determination will pay off in your outer surroundings as you keep attracting better and better outcomes.

Affirmation:

I am always aware of the power of my thoughts, and I use it wisely.

Day 343

The most beautiful thing we can experience is the mysterious. It is the source of all true art and science.

- Albert Einstein

Are you generally comfortable with the "mysterious" aspects of your existence? Are you okay with not knowing everything? Especially when it comes to attracting abundance with the Law of Attraction, it's important to be open to whatever may come as a result of improving your thoughts. You may have some ideas about how your increased abundance will arrive, but what if the universe has other, better ideas?

If you stay focused only on one way money can come to you, you will be blocking all other possibilities, and manifesting your desire may take a lot longer. On the other hand, if you keep affirming your willingness to be open and flexible on "how" it all comes about, you will gain access to a world of endless exciting options that you probably never would have thought of on your own. In effect, you will be giving the universe permission to surprise and thrill you.

Affirmation:

I am open to receive abundance in wonderful unexpected ways.

Day 344

Anyone who doesn't take truth seriously in small matters cannot be trusted in large ones either.

- Albert Einstein

Attracting more abundance into your life depends on your ability to shift your beliefs about two key things: your own self-image, and the nature of abundance itself. Albert Einstein talks about "truths" in his quote above, and when it comes to the Law of Attraction, whatever you believe to be true is what will become your reality. What are your truths about your own self-image? Do you believe that you don't deserve abundance? Do you believe that you will never amount to much? Or do you believe that you are worthy of having everything you desire in life?

What about your truths about abundance itself? Do you believe that receiving abundance has to be hard? Do you believe that the universe is somehow punishing you by withholding your abundance? Or do you believe without a shred of doubt that abundance will flow into your life when you get your thoughts, feelings and beliefs in alignment with it? Your beliefs have immense power in constructing exactly the type of reality you expect to see.

Affirmation:

I choose my truths by believing what I want to be real.

Day 345

If you can't make it better, you can laugh at it.

- Erma Bombeck

Have you ever encountered a situation that you couldn't seem to improve no matter what you did? Has this happened in relation to your money or finances? If so, you know the immense frustration that such a blockage can cause. Most people will simply grit their teeth and bear it until they can figure out a way to fix it, but Erma Bombeck offers a different approach – laugh at it. That may sound ridiculous because there usually isn't anything funny about financial struggle, but in a Law of Attraction context it makes perfect sense.

Laughing at a problem or obstacle does two important things: First, it diffuses the pressure you were feeling as you tried to force solutions that didn't work. When you stop trying to fix it, you immediately start to feel better about it because you release the resistance you were feeling about it. Secondly, laughter lightens your energetic frequency so that you begin broadcasting a better signal to the universe – which will start drawing something better back to you, like a solution to the very problem you are laughing at.

Affirmation:

Laughing at my challenges instantly reduces their power.

Day 346

Spread love everywhere you go. Let no one ever come to you without leaving happier.

- Mother Teresa

Mother Teresa has highlighted one of the keys to great abundance: making sure that you are spreading love everywhere you go. The concept actually applies to much more than just love – you can spread value, appreciation, support, encouragement, and many other great qualities, and you will open the floodgates for abundance to pour in. This is especially true if you apply the concept to your job or business.

The more value you give to people, the more satisfied they will be and the more abundance will flow to you in response. This can happen as a result of satisfied customers spreading the word about you and attracting even more customers; or it can happen in a much less direct way like the universe lining you up with potential partners and opportunities. No matter how it happens, the important thing is to make it a habit to give as much value (or love, or other good qualities) to everyone you can – then watch the magic happen.

Affirmation:

My goal is to spread as much goodness as I can to everyone I meet.

Day 347

Creativity is a natural extension of our enthusiasm.

– Earl Nightingale

Have you ever noticed that creative ideas only come to you when you are feeling positive? When you feel overwhelmed, anxious, frustrated or weary, you simply can't access the creative inspiration because you are on a completely different frequency than it is. This is a great insight to have because it means that simply by putting in the time and effort to improve your mood and generate a little enthusiasm you will immediately start drawing forth creative inspiration.

You can use this creative inspiration in many different ways, from seeking a solution to a problem, to coming up with new business venture ideas, to gaining clarity about your relationships. Regardless how you apply it, the whole process is about working in partnership with the universe to co-create your best life. You simply have to be the one to initiate the partnership by coming into energetic alignment with the abundance and goodness you desire.

Affirmation:

I open my mind to enthusiasm and creative insight.

Day 348

Faith means living with uncertainty - feeling your way through life, letting your heart guide you like a lantern in the dark.

- Dan Millman

One of the common obstacles people encounter along their journey to great abundance is the uncertainty of how it will all come together. This only becomes a problem for people who are in the habit of trying to control everything in their outer environment. Rather than being open to abundance from many sources, they set their sights on a specific source and try to use the Law of Attraction to make money flow through that one source.

Have you done this too? It's understandable to latch onto one apparent source of abundance, because you often can't see any other options. However, the universe can. By channeling all of your energy toward one specific way, you end up closing yourself off from the many other options that would otherwise be possible. Today, start affirming that you are open to wonderful, unexpected surprises that bring all forms of abundance your way. Listen to your heart and follow where it leads – there will be a pot of gold in a place you least expected to find it.

Affirmation:

I embrace uncertainty and open my heart to unexpected abundance.

Day 349

Attitude is Everything, so pick a good one!

- Wayne Dyer

Your overall attitude is of utmost importance as you work consciously with the Law of Attraction, because you will consistently receive outcomes and experiences that are in line with it. Occasional progress is possible even without adjusting your attitude, but it will come in fits and starts and likely make you feel frustrated more than anything else. To achieve consistent results, be sure to focus consistently on attitude improvement.

What kind of improvement? Adjusting your focus from pessimism to optimism, impatience to patience, anger to love, doubt to faith, negative expectations to positive expectations. These adjustments must apply to all areas of your life, not just the acquisition of money and abundance. Focus on improving the quality of your relationships, career, physical well-being, inner peace and spirituality, and so on. This may seem like a lot of work, but the payoff is that abundance in endless forms will then flow easily to you, even if you don't actively visualize it.

Affirmation:

I consciously choose a positive attitude each and every day.

Day 350

To think a thought is an act of creation. If we clothe this thought in feeling, activate it with a strong desire to have it become manifest, the thought or idea begins to take form, to grow like a seed, to attract to itself the conditions, opportunities, resources and all the events necessary to enable its reproduction in our so-called material world.

- Harold Sherman

Harold Sherman shares two important insights about manifesting with his quote above. Many people make the mistake of trying to manifest abundance purely on a mental level. They think about having more money but they fail to infuse those thoughts with the power of emotion. Emotion (especially positive emotion) is like adding fuel to the fire of creation. Focus on something with immense joy, excitement and enthusiasm, and it will manifest more quickly than merely thinking about it.

Also important is having a strong desire for more money. Most of us are trained not to want anything because we might be disappointed if we don't get it. However, the emotion of desire – that deep, yearning feeling – is immensely powerful in drawing the object of our desire to us. Believing it is possible and anticipating its arrival lends even more power to the process. Be sure to infuse your desires with emotional energy and strong desire, rather than simply "thinking" about them.

Affirmation:

Positive emotion and strong desire give life to my dreams and goals.

Day 351

Apparently there is nothing that cannot happen today.

 — Mark Twain

Perhaps Mark Twain was being sarcastic with his comment above, but when you have actively used the Law of Attraction to improve your life, you get used to "miracles" occurring at every turn and you come to believe that indeed, anything and everything is possible. Before you reach that point, however, you may be in the habit of dismissing possibilities because they seem farfetched. "Nah," you say, "that couldn't happen, it would be too good to be true."

Not surprisingly, this "nay say" attitude only creates self-fulfilling prophecies. The good news is that you can just as easily create a "yea say" attitude by deliberately believing that anything is possible. Keep affirming to yourself that yes, this could happen, and yes, that could happen — in fact anything at all can happen, and it can happen far more quickly and easily than you might believe. The universe has untold resources and methods for wowing you — but only if you are willing to allow it.

Affirmation:

Today I choose to believe that everything is possible.

Day 352

Even the most impossible becomes possible, when you are fully released on it. And you know when you are fully released on it when you don't give a hoot. Never suppress feelings. You don't have to satisfy them, but don't suppress them. Just know that they are there, and let go of them.

– Lester Levenson

Lester Levenson's quote above shares a great reminder about the importance of releasing your desires to the universe rather than obsessing and fretting about them. The more you cling to something, the more energy of "lack" you infuse into the creation process, and the longer it will take to arrive. But how can you let go of something that you desire so deeply? It is usually an ongoing process, not something you do just once.

Several times a day get into the habit of consciously letting go of your desire for more abundance (and anything else you are in the process of attracting). Say to yourself, "I let go of this desire and affirm that it will return to me fully formed with perfect timing." Then, during the course of the day if you start feeling needy or worried about your desire not being manifest, repeat the same process again. The more detached you can be the lighter you will feel, and the faster your desire can be formed and delivered.

Affirmation:

It's okay to let go and trust.

Day 353

All power is from within and therefore under our control.

– Robert Collier

Sometimes it may seem as if you have no control over your outer circumstances, especially where money is concerned. Problems and challenges have a way of sneaking up on you when you least expect them, and they can be intimidating enough that you feel completely powerless to change them. It can be helpful to remind yourself that these impressions are merely illusions and you always have the power to turn any situation around. However, long lasting change will not result from trying to change the outer conditions directly.

Outer conditions can only change as a result of going within and creating brand new conditions from your place of inner power. As you withdraw your focus from financial struggle, it starts to fade. As you fantasize about financial ease and freedom, it starts to grow and flow toward you. The more you direct your focus deliberately and consistently, the more you'll notice the outer conditions changing spontaneously – simply because you have accessed your inner power and directed it toward an outcome you desire.

Affirmation:

The power to change anything is already within me.

Day 354

Imagination is your preview of life's coming events.

- Albert Einstein

As Albert Einstein says, imagining something is just like seeing a preview of a coming event – you can actually create amazing life experiences just by imagining them! If you are like many other people, however, your imagination might be a little bit rusty. Do you sometimes have trouble imagining great scenes for your life? If so, try the following exercise. Before you try to imagine anything in detail, grab a sheet of paper and a pen, and jot down some ideas for neat experiences you would love to have.

Don't worry about these things being possible or not – simply concoct the coolest, most exciting fantasies you can think of and write them down. Then, spend at least 10 minutes quieting your mind and relaxing your body. When you feel ready, glance at your list and start imagining the first scenario. Don't try to direct it too much, just imagine how great it would be for that to happen, and slip into a daydream state of mind as you engage with the essence of the experiences. Not only will you enjoy the process, you'll get better at it the more you do it.

Affirmation:

I allow my imagination to roam far and wide.

Day 355

Be like water making its way through cracks. Do not be assertive, but adjust to the object, and you shall find a way round or through it. If nothing within you stays rigid, outward things will disclose themselves.

- Bruce Lee

Bruce Lee's advice above offers a great approach for dealing with obstacles in life, but it's also a great way to work with the Law of Attraction to manifest abundance in your life. Most of us tend to go the opposite way: we're tense, irritable, forceful and impatient. If it won't work on its own, we'll make it work gosh darn it. Not surprisingly, this rigid, aggressive attitude can only attract to us more and more obstacles that seem to bar our way. If we follow Bruce Lee's advice and simply relax, let go and flow, we often find that the obstacles dissolve of their own volition.

Even if they don't completely dissolve, our open, flexible state of mind helps us to recognize solutions and alternate routes to our goal so we can bypass the obstacles easily. The most challenging aspect of this technique is breaking the habit of force. If this is a problem for you, simply keep repeating mentally, "Be like water; let go and flow" and before long you will have developed a much more relaxed attitude to help you manifest abundance more easily.

Affirmation:

I choose to be flexible, relaxed and fluid.

Day 356

Sometimes your joy is the source of your smile, but sometimes your smile can be the source of your joy.

-Thich Nhat Hanh

Regularly adopting a joyful, positive state of mind is vital in attracting more abundance into your life, but sometimes it can seem like a monumental task to accomplish this. Especially if you have a lot of "unpleasantness" in certain areas of your life, you may struggle to find anything to feel joyful or happy about. Believe it or not, just smiling for no reason can often be a great trigger for lightening your mood.

Studies have shown that the very act of smiling can make you feel happier, because you stimulate the facial muscles that are associated with pleasant emotions, like happiness. Try it sometime! Simply smile the biggest, widest, happiest grin you can muster. You can even think about something that makes you feel happy or something that makes you laugh. Then pay close attention to your feelings and you should notice that you feel a bit lighter and more positive.

Affirmation:

Smiling connects me to the essence of abundance.

Day 357

All happenings, great and small, are parables whereby God speaks. The art of life is to get the message.

- Malcolm Muggeridge

Today's quote is a great reminder that everything that happens in your outer environment is really just "feedback" from the universe regarding your past thoughts and beliefs. When something negative happens, it's a great opportunity to reflect on the possible reasons for it. Which of your habitual thoughts, beliefs or expectations could have attracted it? Remember that these thoughts do not have to be literal. You do not need to have imagined something precisely in order to receive it – but you were focused on something that contained the same essence.

Once you have an idea of which mindset may have triggered the manifestation, then you have a new objective: to turn that mindset around pronto! Just because you've received an unwanted manifestation does not mean it's too late to improve the situation. It simply means that you are being given a chance to heal your erroneous thought patterns and create something better from this point on. Over time, using this technique can help you clear many unhealthy beliefs and achieve greater levels of abundance and peace in all areas of your life.

Affirmation: Everything around me is simply a reflection of my dominant mindset.

Day 358

Enjoy doing nothing without falling asleep - meditation.

- J. Kleykamp

Regular rest and rejuvenation is crucial in developing an abundance mindset, but it's also something that many of us tend to resist. Whether we don't recognize the importance of it, we have too many other "important" things to do, or we feel we don't deserve some downtime, too many of us deprive our minds and bodies of the rest they need. Unfortunately, this has a negative impact on our ability to attract abundance because during the course of our busyness we absorb a lot of stress and negativity.

Daily meditation is one good way to start turning this around – and it doesn't have to complicated or time consuming. As today's quote reveals, you can simply take a few minutes a day to "enjoy doing nothing". Sitting quietly with your eyes closed and focusing on your breathing is a great way to release stress and strengthen your inner spiritual connection again. Doing this regularly helps you to detach from negative influences and connect more easily with the essence of abundance – thereby attracting more of it effortlessly.

Affirmation:

I give myself permission to relax and recharge daily.

Day 359

When any fit of anxiety or gloominess or perversion of the mind lays hold upon you, make it a rule not to publish it by complaints but exert your whole care to hide it. By endeavoring to hide it, you will drive it away.

-Dr. Samuel Johnson

Are you in the habit of complaining to other people about the problems of your life? Do you and your friends get together and swap woes? Activities like this can only strengthen expressions of negativity in your life because you are actually lending power to them the more you complain about them. Your focus on the problem begins to draw more of that essence into your life, and then by voicing your complaints you reinforce the "reality" that makes you so unhappy.

Dr. Samuel Johnson offers an unusual remedy in today's quote: hide your displeasure. However, he may not mean that exactly as you think. Rather than bottling up your negative feelings but continuing to stew about the problem internally, you can simply practice "dropping it" – mentally, verbally and emotionally. Hide it, not only from others but also yourself. Refuse to dwell on it. Refuse to speak about it. Refuse to think about it at all if you can help it, and you will drive it away. It cannot grow and thrive if it is not fed with energy and attention.

Affirmation: Rather than complaining, I choose to voice positive expectations.

Day 360

Money will come when you are doing the right thing.

- Mike Phillips

This quote by Mike Phillips seems to point to taking the right actions to attract money into our lives, but we might also see it in a different light and deepen the meaning. What do you think the "right things" would be when it comes to having plenty of money? Working hard, doing what you love, giving to the needy, and knowing you deserve abundance are a good start.

Here's one more you may not have considered: Integrity. "Doing the right thing" can also mean treating others with the same respect you would expect for yourself, providing as much value as you possibly can in your job or business, and otherwise conducting your life from a place of high values. When you do so every action, every thought, every deed attracts like results back to you.

Affirmation:

What I put out into the world always comes back to me.

Day 361

There is only one success: to be able to spend your life in your own way.

- Christopher Morley

Most of us tend to equate success with outer manifestations like money, cars, dream homes, and the like. Christopher Morley reminds us that there is an even bigger benefit of success: the freedom to live your best life on all levels. When we stop to think about it, we realize that there are many people in the world who have all the outer trappings of wealth and success but still aren't happy, simply because they are not living life on their own terms.

We would do well to figure out exactly what success and abundance mean to us - both inner and outer manifestations of them - and then model our goals and dreams after those ideals. Having plenty of money and material wealth is a blessing – but it shouldn't be our ultimate goal in life. Much more important is feeling truly satisfied and fulfilled by the big picture of our life.

Affirmation:

My inner satisfaction is reflected as outer abundance.

Day 362

You can have everything you want if you help enough other people get what they want.

- Zig Ziglar

These famous words by Zig Ziglar are often misinterpreted to mean that we should focus all of our attention on helping others, even sacrificing our own stability in the process. However, when we consider that Mr. Ziglar was a brilliant salesperson, we can see clearly that isn't the example he set with his own success.

Rather than seeing this quote as an exercise in charity, we can grasp a deeper meaning about our own skills, talents, and dreams – and the ways we can use them to help others live better lives. Helping people get what they want means simply offering what we have to share and allowing it to benefit others while also benefiting ourselves, monetarily or otherwise.

Affirmation:

I have a lot to offer the world.

Day 363

Reach high, for stars lie hidden in your soul. Dream deep, for every dream precedes a goal.

- Pamela Vaull Starr

This poetic quote by Pamela Vaull Starr shares great insight into the magic of believing in ourselves and our dreams. Do you really believe that "stars lie hidden in your soul"? You might think of these stars as seeds of potential – but they cannot bloom into magnificence if you remain content to leave them in a dormant state.

The second part of the quote is especially illuminating because it reminds us that our dreams cannot be about "surface stuff" – they must be deep and meaningful to us. They must get our heart racing, mind reeling and our creative juices flowing. Otherwise they are just nice ideas – but not motivating enough for us to take action on them.

Affirmation:

The intensity of my excitement reveals the depth of my goal.

Day 364

Destiny is not a matter of chance; it's a matter of choice.

- Unknown

Choice is something that many of us forget we have, and it goes way beyond the mundane decisions that make up our day to day lives. Most of us make decisions based on a preconceived framework of limitations. We believe we must choose between this job or that job, but total financial freedom is out of our reach; or we can earn an income between "this much and that much", but definitely not more than that.

The funny thing about making firm decisions is that it usually calls forth the resources to meet the demands. If we were to make a firm decision to earn one million dollars a year and hold to that vision, we would find our circumstances shifting and opportunities arriving to make it possible. That doesn't mean we wouldn't have to work for it, but just knowing that we have the power to choose what we really want despite apparent limitations can be life-changing.

Affirmation:

I can choose to create anything I desire.

Day 365

What I know for sure is that what you give comes back to you.

- Oprah Winfrey

Oprah Winfrey is a prime example of the power of conceiving a higher purpose – and the rich rewards that come from doing so. Oprah has publicly stated that she asked the universe to use her for a higher purpose, then followed where she felt she was being led. As she did this, one success built upon another until she had created an empire of television and radio shows, a magazine, and many other vehicles to share her gifts with the world.

Even if you have no desire to become as famous as Oprah Winfrey, you may want to ponder her approach and consider how you can apply the same concept in your own life. Think about your own talents, gifts and skills, and ask for guidance about the best ways to share them with others. Ask to be led to the best opportunities, and then simply take one step at a time in creating the gateways through which your wealth can be delivered.

Affirmation:

The universe richly rewards me for sharing my gifts with the world.

ABOUT THE AUTHOR

Valerie Dawson, known as the 'Mindset Mentor' has helped thousands of people to achieve their life goals. She has combined her unique background in psychology, hypnosis and life coaching into her breakthrough program, *'The Dawson Method'*. To learn more about Valerie's programs, visit her website: www.MagneticMindset.com

Printed in Great Britain
by Amazon